European Perspectives
on
Hispanic Literature
of the
United States

edited by
Genvieve Fabre

Arte Publico Press
Houston

This volume is made possible through support from the Université Paris VII and the Centre Interdisciplinaire de Recherches Nord-Americaines. The articles included in this volume were selected from papers given at the 1986 International Conference on "Hispanic Cultures and Identities in the United States" held in Paris in 1986.

Arte Publico Press
University of Houston
Houston, Texas 77004

LC   87-73034
ISBN 0-934770-84-0

Copyright © 1988 by Arte Publico Press
Printed in the United States of America

Contents

Introduction: Blueprints in the Development of a New Poetics, *by Genvieve Fabre*
"A midnight reality": Puerto Rican Poetry in New York, a Poetry of Dreams, *by Wolfgang Binder*
Ricardo Sánchez: The Poetics of Liberation, *by Yves-Charles Grandjeat*
The Recovery of Nineteenth Century Chicano Autobiography, *by Genaro Padilla*
Mediators and Mediation in Rudolfo Anaya's Trilogy: *Bless Me, Ultima, Heart of Aztlán* and *Tortuga*, *by Jean Cazemajou*
The Establishment of Community in Zora Neale Hurston's *The Eatonville Anthology* (1926) and Rolando Hinojosa's *Estampas el valle* (1973), *by Heiner Bus*
Myth, Identity and Struggle in Three Chicano Novels: Aztlán . . . Anaya, Méndez, Acosta, *by Alurista*
Code-Switching as Metaphor in Chicano Poetry, *by Cordelia Candelaria*
Homosexuality and the Chicano Novel, *by Bruce-Novoa*
Internal Exile in the Chicano Novel: Structure and Paradigms, *by Francisco A. Lomelí*
Chicano and Nuyorican Literature—Elements of a Democratic and Socialist Culture in the U.S. of A?, *by Dieter Herms*
The Chicana: A Marginal Woman, *by Marcienne Rocard*
Cultural Ambivalence in Early Chicana Literature, *by Gloria Velázquez Treviño*
La Vida Es un Spanglish Disparatero: Bilingualism in Nuyorican Poetry, *by Frances R. Aparicio*

Introduction
Blueprints in the Development of a New Poetics

Genvieve Fabre
Université Paris VII

Over the last ten years French students and scholars have expressed a sustained and genuine interest in the Hispanic communities of the United States. Efforts have been made to acquire documentation—primary and secondary sources—to establish contacts with Hispanic scholars, writers and artists, to introduce their works to French bookstores and university libraries, to include them in the syllabi of certain courses. In 1985 a course was taught at the graduate level in all French universities; on that occasion the University of Bordeaux published a collection of essays (Cazemajou). Today more students are doing research in that field and two Ph.D. dissertations were recently presented at the University of Paris VII (Grandjeat, Menendez). More are in progress.

The March 1986 International Conference on "Hispanic Cultures and Identities in the United States" which was held in Paris was organized in order to promote interest and research in this new field. Individual scholars or poets had been invited to various centers (Toulouse, Bordeaux, Aix and Dijon. . . .) to give readings of their works or to participate in workshops and conferences. The 1986 conference was, however, the first important gathering bringing together European and American scholars, French students and academics, Hispanic critics, artists, writers. We deliberately expanded the theme of earlier European Conferences (in Paris on Puerto Rico in 1975, in Gemersceim, Germany, on Chicanos in 1984). We included discussion on several groups (mostly Mexican Americans, Puerto Ricans and Cubans) in a comparative perspective. Our objective was to attempt to analyze the range and significance of cross-cultural exchanges between the worlds to which each of these communities are related: Latin American, Mexican, Caribbean, North American, Spanish. . . . Although the emphasis was on present trends, we were also interested in tracing historical developments. Finally, the conference was interdisciplinary: it invited specialists from various fields—anthropology, sociology, history, art and literary criticism—to confront each other's theories and points of view. The theme "Hispanic identities and cultures" was controversial since it raised a series of interrogations: on the existence of one or several identities, of similarities or differences between cultures which share linguistic practices but have evolved separate and singular modes of expression. Each group was studied in its relationship to its distinctive past and history, to its homeland, to the United States. We also tried to analyze the conditions of emergence of these communities within American society, the problem they have encountered in their confrontation with a new, often hostile environment, the extent to which they have accepted, refused or controlled their acculturation and, in the process, maintained or relinquished their own cultural traits and reshaped their identity.

In order to answer some of these questions, we examined the role of symbolic acts and structures, of social, moral and collective imagination; we tried to assess the cultural and historical particularity of each group, as well as its cross-cultural and cross-historical accessibility. We turned to the visual art in an attempt to see whether a better understanding of the historical and social reality could be reached through the analysis of the artists' response, through their "interpretive translations." We believe that it is through aesthetic forms that some ways of experiencing are best manifested, that certain things only partially perceived or felt are revealed with eloquence and potency in a work of art, that the artist has a crucial role to play in the interpretation of a culture (Geerts, 1973), in the elaboration, through certain symbolic strategies and complex sign systems, of what has been called "a culture of criticism and a criticism of culture" (Gunn, 1987). We were not so much interested in construing reality "as it is," but in understanding its interpretation, imaginative representation and metaphorization in the works of poets, fiction writers, autobiographers, playwrights, film makers or painters.

Workshops were organized around these various artistic forms so that closer attention could be brought to the specificity of each genre and to the particular methodological approach each necessitated. Individual works were examined, general problems debated, points of views and theoretical frameworks confronted.

Because some writers were present at the Paris conference— Anaya, Elizondo, Alurista, Martín, Barquet, Cofer, Huerta, Bruce-Novoa, Montoya, Castillo. . . . —and because so many writers are also critics, a confrontation took place and a dialogue went on: critics and writers challenged one another, both offering the fundamental instruments and material for a poetics yet to come. On the part of the writers, there has always been a determination to keep out of polemical discussion and a certain resentment or amusement at seeing their writings used as tools for a critical experimentation that often forces the text into exclusive categories and narrow definitions. But, simultaneously, they have expressed a desire to be informed on the latest trends and to help shape the critical sensibility: the task of theorization should not befall the critic exclusively and new theories are often induced by the works themselves. On the part of the critics, attempts are constantly being carried out to work out the principles and methods of a new poetics through a close examination of both the scholarly readings in literary criticism and the creative works. Critics have been first compelled to fight against certain current allegations: that Hispanic literatures in the United States are new and as such are still suffering from immaturity, coarseness of literary devices, lack of sophistication; that they are a by-product of the 1970's political movements, therefore ephemeral and limited to propaganda and protest or condemned to be mostly documentary, testimonial or journalistic. Or this production is seen as a "literature of the oppressed" of the uprooted, exiled communities—still caught up in the immigrant or colonized syndrome and in a culture of poverty.

The first task of Hispanic writers and critics has been to make diverse claims in order to build up new premises from which to proceed toward a fairer appreciation and toward the framing of a new poetics. The flowering of works since the late 1960's entitles these literatures a space in the North American literary scene and commands more than desultory attention. It constitutes an important and recognizable current and perhaps a challenge to the mainstream production. This sudden visibility and vocality of the Hispanic voice, among so many others, can no longer be denied or ignored, and Latinos cannot be satisfied with a minority or subliterature status.

In many ways, these claims parallel those of other groups—Afro-Americans, Asian-Americans, Amerindians—who have been fighting for cultural visibility and literary recognition with similar rhetorical persuasion. The "newly emerging" Hispanic literatures have a historical dimension and are the prolongation of earlier efforts; they have their precursors and pioneers to whom credit must be given; they are also firmly rooted in several traditions (which in some cases can be traced back to pre-Columbian times): Indio, Hispanic, Latin American, Mexican, Caribbean. . . . Quite distinct from other ethnic and European immigrant literatures, they definitely belong to the New World. Present day writers are very conscious of their indebtedness to literary forebears and to specific cultural forms and practices.

The inscription in cultural tradition and in history—a history of conquest and subjugation, of exile, revolution and migration—grants some degree of legitimacy. These traditions have not been servilely followed or reproduced. They have served as testing ground, starting point and fundamental reference; they have been transformed, reinterpreted and recreated. Much scholarly work has been devoted to the writing of literary histories and to the identification of and access to all the material and sources, to establishing bibliographic control and tools. Works forgotten or long ignored have been rescued from oblivion, inventoried and reconstructed, in order to set them in their proper historical perspective and semantic system. G. Padilla's* sustained research on nineteenth-century autobiographical texts has considerably enriched the understanding of the earlier expressive forms and their enduring significance.

In this reconstruction of literary history, the question of origin has come up; it is differently dealt with and is inevitably connected with the problem of terminology—Chicano, Mexican, Mexican-American, Puerto Rican or Nuyorican, Cuban, Latin American, Hispanic or Latino. Each term emphasizes a degree of relatedness to various geocultural areas, national entities or historical periods. For Alurista,* 1848 is for Mexican-Americans, native and immigrated, the most important landmark; and their history is one of resistance to acculturation, and struggle for cultural integrity "to rethink themselves as a whole and meaningful people," relating to the same mythical mother-land, Aztlán. As poet, critic and cultural historian, Alurista demonstrates the thrust of this myth of origin, its use as a unifying metaphor, even if it is constantly being reinterpreted by Mexican and Chicano authors. Treviño,* examining early Chicana writing (Mena and Gonzalez) argues against the common assumption that these precursors are assimilationist, tame and imitative, romantic and pastoral. She proceeds to show that they are less descriptive than critical and interpretive, and are mostly concerned with contrasting Mexican and Anglo-American cultures.

Mainland Puerto-Rican literature has been likewise analyzed through the various stages of its development. With its early attachment to national—island—and to Latin American cultures, its sense of vulnerability to the American environment, its indictment of the colonial situation, it grew form a Puerto Rican literature written in Spanish into a Proto-Nuyorican, then to a full-fledged actively bilingual Nuyorican art from (Flores). Historians of both Cuban and Puerto-Rican literatures in the United States (Binder,* Hasson,* Martin,* Barquet*) have emphasized the role of early exiles who established an important literary community and created works first inspired by their rejection of Spanish rule, but demonstrated their strong links to the "national" culture. In the process of becoming "main land"—whatever the reasons, ideological, political, economic, for the artists' separation from their initial homelands—these literatures have still retained strong ties with the islands and with their Caribbean settings. Closer examination of the respective history of both Puerto Rican and Cuban communities would of course highlight many differences beyond these fundamental similarities.

Scholars looking at the early history have also insisted on the—too often neglected—importance of orality. That verbal culture, musically and orally transmitted, has been and still is a constant inspiration for writers; popular singers—creators of jibaro music, plenas and boleros—storytellers, their toasts, ballads and corridos, have been the real pioneers and speechmakers, and form a genuine and integral part of the artistic production. The speaking and singing voice has paved the way for the written word, suggested a wealth of rhymes and rhythms, and many of the so-called literary devices have been shaped by orality—as is demonstrated in this volume by Portelli's* study of Pietri's poetry. Portelli draws attention to the call and response pattern which has been equally important for Black and Nuyorican poets, to the influence of music, the interplay of sounds and signs, names and spelling. He also shows how oral forms transferred to new contexts assume new significance, and how the confrontation between the flexible signs of orality and the more frozen ones of institutional writing can generate tensions; writing has "expropriated the spoken word of power and relevance." These verbal cultures, never granted recognition by the dominant print culture, are now acknowledged by Hispanic writers—as they have been by Afro-Americans and Amerindians—as an essential and legitimate source of inspiration, as well as enduring artistic forms. Singers and composers like Hernandez, Flores, Romito . . . sing about the Puerto Rican community of New York and their performances belong to the strong expressive modes of the Nuyorican poetry.

Perhaps something should be said here about visual arts which were discussed in one of the workshops of the Paris conference (by Nieto, Marchand, Zamudio, Pinke, Ybarra-Frausto, Luis), about the complex dialectical sign and symbol system stemming from popular culture they have created. One could also suggest that the interaction between visual and oral art forms and written literatures be further explored.

Surely writers should not be separated from the broader artistic community of bards, musicians and painters. Through different media they are all struggling to transfer and transform the raw material of experience into a creative art which also expresses their critical response to United States society. Furthermore we should note that the similarities between Afro-Americans' and the various Latino groups' literary histories have encouraged openness and artistic interchange. A poet like Alurista is very much aware of the wealth of imagery, rhythm and rhetorical devices to be found in black poetry of the 1960's, and the Nuyoricans' poetic work has always been close to that of the black poets. One could find many more examples of those affinities: they should not be explored in terms of indebtedness, influence or imitation, but should rather be seen as an active creative interaction. These interactions may or may not be consciously pursued; they nevertheless exist on many levels. One could venture to say that—theoretically and ideologically—Puerto Ricans and Afro-Cubans feel more keyed to the Afro-American sensibility, whereas Chicanos are more willing to admit their affinity with the Indian heritage, an affinity which will perhaps elicit among them a greater curiosity for Amerindian literature.

A European observer may be more interested in tracing the history of all these interchanges (Bus,* for instance, in his comparative study of Zora Neale Hurston's work and Rolando Hinojosa's) than the Hispanic critics, perhaps because for them the critical issue is the identification of their cultures and literatures, the definition of genuinely specific "Chicano," "Puerto Rican" or "Cuban" traits. Identification has been a leit motiv among critics and a definite task, and just as the reconstruction of literary history, it touches upon many important issues. One is struck by some paradoxical and highly polemical aspects of this search for identification criteria. Its immediate and most urgent goal is to set definite boundaries, emphasize the uniqueness. This has been an ongoing process among North American ethnic literatures eager to claim their own space and identity. The titles of so many books, collections of essays, anthologies testify to that trend. On the other hand, these literatures, which have become more visible and more productive in the last two decades, share some characteristics. The communality of political messages and expressive forms has been pointed out by mainstream as well as by the "ethnic" critics. Hispanic critics, when trying to enumerate specific features, have been forced into certain categorization and theorization which could also apply to other groups; the findings of each set of critics in their quest for an appropriate methodological framework could easily be used and transferred to a body of works for which it was not initially meant. Each—Afro-American, Puerto Rican, Chicano, Amerindian—have contributed to the shaping of a "Method" for the analysis of ethnic cultures, while trying simultaneously to build up a Black, Chicano, etc. aesthetics. This setting up and leveling of ethnic boundaries is significant of what is now happening in the literary world of the United States, a society which on the one hand is still eager to define the canons of its Americanness—still groping for a fundamental national unity and identity distinct from that of its

Canadian, Mexican, Latin American or Caribbean neighbors or from its European forebears—and on the other hand is equally aware of its pluriethnic composition. This multi-ethnic character has been forced to its attention in an unprecedented way by the various "movements" of the '60s and '70s. But the more recent emergence of gay and feminist movements has again erected new boundaries while erasing others; they have introduced internal divisions at the same time as they have created cross-cultural bonds. In the North American context, in which so many new cultures and cultural forms are emerging, ethnic boundaries are in a state of constant flux.

In their search for identification, Hispanics have been compelled to assert their difference both from mainstream America and from their original cultural matrices or the national entities from which they have been exiled or estranged. The whole process of their historical development, together with the perception that American dominant society imposes upon them, forces them into ambiguous and contradictory strategies: on the one hand toward assimilation and admittance into the literary canons, toward a struggle against discrimination and entrenchment into inferiority (minority or immigrant) status; on the other hand toward recognition of their distinctive ethnic traits, acknowledgement of their right to be different, of their will to remain unassimilated and to create an original and "new" artistic expression. Integration or autonomy, acceptance of norms set by others or self-determination: these two trends are to be found in the literary criticism and in the production itself and may coexist in the same work.

Just as the Afro-American critics—Stepto, Gates, Baker et al (Gates, 1984)—, Hispanic critics are claiming the right to use, for the analysis of their literatures, the same elaborate tools as those used for legitimate mainstream production. Derrida, Bataille, Deleuze, Riffaterre, Foucault and many others who have become authorities in literary scholarship (with its strange Eurocentric bias) are called upon and repeatedly quoted. Yet another ongoing argument is that each ethnic literature has developed its distinctive aesthetics and is best analyzed by a member of the community who has an inside knowledge of the culture; outsiders, whatever their capacities as critics, will never grasp the total significance of the work; the Hispanic critic and reader then become the indispensable mediators and interpreters.

The whole issue of interpretation is posed here. At the pre sent stage, we are facing a situation in which Hispanics have proved that they were best equipped for the task; they have sharpened their tools and their perspectives, and are offering a "creative understanding" that no outsider could hope to match. It is also a situation in which, with a few exceptions, Chicanos tend to discuss mostly Chicano work, Puerto Rican Puerto Rican work, etc., and boundaries and competitiveness seem quite strong here. Several questions may be raised: What degree of interchange goes on in a Latino conference where all the groups are present, each very much aware of the other but fairly confined to the exploration of its own territory? What comes out of a conference like the Paris conference or any European event where Hispanics confront distanced observers? What can be an outsider's contribution to a better understanding and assessment?

The allegations, judgments or the silence of the American (mainstream) literary establishment have certainly encouraged many to believe that on some occasions the outsider's point of view could be prejudicial and harmful. On the other hand, cultural and interpretive anthropology has recently focused its attention on the concept of otherness; and exotopy—a term coined by Todorov in his discussion of Bakhtin's ideas (Bakhtin, 1981)—is presented as "the most powerful lever of understanding. It is only through the eye of another culture that the alien culture reveals itself more completely and more deeply—but never exhaustively." Bakhtin's principle of dialectical exteriority challenges many current assumptions. In calling for a "dialogics of culture," he shows how to use our own historical and cultural exotopy to understand that of another. In setting the guidelines for a creative interpretation of culture and a better comprehension of the place of alterity, Bakhtin further analyzes the culturally mediated process of interaction and transaction between reader and text, which involves both distanciation and appropriation. But he maintains that the otherness of the text is not so much overcome by reading as grasped by being made conversable: "the dialogics principle." The aim of interpretation is not to absorb alterity but to fathom it by deepening the dialogue both about and with the distance, the strangeness, the difference it implies. We find an echo of this idea in Geertz (1983), his wonders "how deeply different can be deeply known without becoming any less different, the enormously distant enormously close without becoming any less farther away."

Al Leal and Lomelí have pointed out (Jimenez, 1979, Leal et al, 1982), the very controversial question or identification and interpretation remains unsolved; yet a combination of indicators can be used, none being an absolute criterion in itself. Authorship, if it is assumed that Hispanic literature is not only *about* Hispanics but *by* Hispanics. The origin of the work can also be detected through its representation of a special experience and sensibility, in characters and in situations, through the language, tone and world view. It can also be assessed in terms of "conscientizacio," of its socio-political message, or through its specific historical references. It can finally be grasped through its imaginative and symbolic structure. Readership remains a crucial issue. Destined primarily to its own ethnic community, the work must relate to those privileged readers; but it may also wish to reach a more diversified audience and its whole sign system has to be constructed to meet these different goals. Reality must be reinterpreted through artistic modes that are keyed to the distinct experience and sensibility but also assume some kind of general significance. The claim to universality is much debated and there is no agreement on the relationship between the ethnic character of a work and its universal appeal. Is "ethnicity" to be considered as an obstacle? Or does the thorough exploration of an ethnic reality necessarily open out to the revelation of universal values?

The essays presented in this volume help further expand the conceptual framework within which Hispanic literatures can be apprehended. One is struck by the recurrence of certain notions from one critical text to the other, whatever the perspective it chooses to work from. A first set of notions is centered around the identification of experience, stressing either the negative side (the drift, estrangement and uprootedness, the fragmentation, the frustrations and the entrapments) or the positive aspects which the ordeal may lead to (*defiance, sense or purpose, awareness, control, search for identity, liberation, spiritual growth. . . .) The commitment here is to the study of literature as the study of men in their historical changes or a study of their changing views of reality. The role of literature is to explore—formally—the experience of these changes. Whether critics insist that the fundamental issue is the experience of reality in its changing forms or the formal changes in the reality of experience—changes that literature can mediate if it breaks free from mimetic conventions—the focus of attention is still the experience. Nieto, in her examination of Carlos Almarez's pictorial work, analyzed the dialectics between experience and memory, life and death, violence and conflict. Rocard* stressed the urgency of self definition and assertion and relates the genesis and ordeal of Mexican-American women. Rizk emphasized the struggle to resist assimilation among Hispanic play-wrights and poets and their still unresolved search for identity. Lomelí* explored the theme of exile and isolation—enhanced by the rejection of society—and shows how it has acquired new modes of expression. The sense of non-conformity, the posture chosen by some writers (Rios, de Casas and Cardenas), is transformed into "registers of authentic expression" resisting labels that infringe upon the quest of personal identity. Grandjeat* studied the passage from serf to self, the overcoming of a sense of dislocation and argued of its socio-political message, or through its specific historical references. It can finally be grasped through its imaginative and symbolic structure. Readership remains a crucial issue. Destined primarily to its own ethnic community, the work must relate to those privileged readers; but it may also wish to reach a more diversified audience and its whole sign system has to be constructed to meet these different goals. Reality must be reinterpreted through artistic modes that are keyed to the distinct experience and sensibility but also assume some kind of general significance. The claim to universality is much debated and there is no agreement on the relationship between the ethnic character of a work and its universal appeal. Is "ethnicity" to be considered as an obstacle? Or does the thorough exploration of an ethnic reality necessarily open out to the revelation of universal values?

The essays presented in this volume help further expand the conceptual framework within which Hispanic literatures can be apprehended. One is struck by the recurrence of certain notions from one critical text to the other, whatever the perspective it chooses to work from. A first set of notions is centered around the identification of experience, stressing either the negative side (the drift, estrangement and uprootedness, the fragmentation, the frustrations and the entrapments) or the positive aspects which the ordeal may lead to (*defiance, sense or purpose, awareness, control, search for identity, liberation, spiritual growth. . . .) The commitment here is to the study of literature as the study of men in their historical changes or a study of their changing views of reality. The role of literature is to explore—formally—the experience of these changes. Whether critics insist that the fundamental issue is the experience of reality in its changing forms or the formal changes in the reality of experience—changes that literature can mediate if it breaks free from mimetic conventions—the focus of attention is still the experience. Nieto, in her examination of Carlos Almarez's pictorial work, analyzed the dialectics between experience and memory, life and death, violence and conflict. Rocard* stressed the urgency of self definition and assertion and relates the genesis and ordeal of Mexican-American women. Rizk emphasized the struggle to resist assimilation among Hispanic play-wrights and poets and their still unresolved search for identity. Lomelí* explored the theme of exile and isolation—enhanced by the rejection of society—and shows how it has acquired new modes of expression. The sense of non-conformity, the posture chosen by some writers (Rios, de Casas and Cardenas), is transformed into "registers of authentic expression" resisting labels that infringe upon the quest of personal identity. Grandjeat* studied the passage from serf to self, the overcoming of a sense of dislocation and argued inner and outer space, between individual thrust and collective dynamics; the theme of exile (and internal exile) and return, are being constantly explored. What is emphasized here is the precarious and institutionalized marginality—through the "edge" and the "fringe" images—the transience and what Edward Shils (1981) has called the "unchartedness of the world." Bruce-Novoa* stressed the hidden and secret aspects of the experience, while other critics insisted more on the historical, geographical perspective most critics have (Treviño* on the Chicana writers), on the definite sense of place evident in most work (Olivares on "the streets in Gary Soto," Cazemajou* on Anaya's trilogy); and Lomelí* developed the concept of geopoetics. All these diversified notions are relevant to literary criticism when analyzed through the various art forms they receive. These forms are usually examined through the convenient although often discredited generic approach—autobiography, fictional or not; novel, short story, poetry, theatre. . . . These genres are apprehended as modes—narrative, lyrical, dramatic . . . —further identified as pastoral, picaresque, romantic, realistic, melodramatic or satirical, as traditional, modern or postmodern. But what really comes under scrutiny are the literary devices—syntactic, structured or semantic—through which art expresses and reinterprets reality (Miguélez,* Alarcón* discussing respectively the narrator's point of view and the mirror symbol).

The method is borrowed from the different schools—formalist and textual or sociological and contextual—with an attempt not to fall into the trap which both extremes may present: avoidance of the social historical dimension of literary discourse on the one hand, yielding to dogmatic ideology on the other. In evolving a new poetics, which uses the elaborate tools of literary scholarship but considers the Hispanic literatures as a separate entity in the field of North American letters, critics have sought to articulate the interdependency of two characteristics of "literary artifacts": their complex formal organization and their status as acts of social communication or political statement. The extent to which each approach has been used and the validity of each school has been thoroughly examined on many occasions (Bruce-Novoa, 1975; Saldívar, 1979; Salazar Parr and Sommers in Jiménes, 1979). Chicano critics have argued for a diversified analytical method that would arise from the object studied and not be artificially fastened on from outside. One is nevertheless struck by the predominance of formalist analysis, with its emphasis on literariness, its attention to paradigm and to archetypal thematic and linguistic devices. The culturalist approach—sometimes called ethnopoetics (Cazemajou*)—more keyed to the identification of experience and culture—has also been deemed essential. It stresses the distinctive features as an expression of the authenticity of the culture. Sommers, however, recommends a more comprehensive method—"dialectical historical"—which considers formal aspects in relation to the broader historical context; a sense of cultural identity fused with critical awareness forces a confrontation with both the dominant society and the "traditional" culture, and sometimes demands a change in both. Saldívar has insisted upon the "dialectics of difference", and recently women critics have highlighted the new feminist perspective which calls for a reexamination of the existing texts, of stereotypes and for the abolition in Chicano culture of elements oppressive to women. In the workshop on feminist and feminine writing in Paris (Buxo y Rey, Lawn, Treviño,* Rocard,* Rebolledo, Herrera-Sobek, Vargas. . . .), the paper of L. Hasson on Lidia Cabrera, or in the discussions Lidia Cabrera, or in the discussions on women dramatists (in the theatre workshop: Kaiser-Lenoir, Rizk. . . .), attention has been brought to the identification of the women's point of view, to the opposition between repressed anger and silences, and to new rhetorical strategies. The issue of homosexuality has also been addressed. Bruce-Novoa, aware of its presence as an overt or underlying theme in Hispanic literatures, suggested new ways of decoding texts in an "infrastructural" level. The distinctive artistic sensibility stemming from this historical situation and the entanglement with a long-standing tradition, the new wealth of imagery, motifs and themes brought by these viewpoints is now seen as an indispensable contribution to the aesthetic.

If one combines the findings of each different approach, one can bring out the main tenets of a poetics which—with varying degree of attention to text or context—is essentially concerned with defining the specificity of the Hispanic literary discourse.

The act of writing—as for many other "ethnic" writers and I think particularly of Afro-American writers (Gates, 1984)—is seen as the result of a fiery determination to break the silence, to affirm what has been denied or negated, to reorder experience and forge—artistically—a collective identity. The structure of most works is described as dialectical, based upon tensions between two ways of perceiving reality and values, and a binary pattern of opposites brought by the interaction between different cultures but also between class, sex, race, generation. This determines the semantic space of the literature as the "intersection of the cultural historical reality appropriated by the text to produce itself and the aesthetic reality produced by the text" (Saldívar in Jiménez, 1979). The dialectics is also the result of a paradoxical impulse to destroy and to reconstruct. In that perspective many works written from a "subversive edge" are seen as the production of an ideology of difference. In defining its canon, the poetic emphasizes the aesthetic and spiritual character of Hispanic culture as opposed to the more materialistic technological majority culture. In the literary space created by art, the national and ethnic identities are held apart but are also related by intricate bonds. Image retrieving, to recreate fragments of memory to resist chaotic discontinuity or threats of destruction, is an essential activity (Bruce-Novoa, 1975). Events, figures have to be rescued from oblivion, restored to visibility. Writing as asserted as an act of survival—the affirmation of the vitality of culture and the will to endure in the face of all odds—an act of liberation—from the temptation of assimilation, of silence, from partial or total annihilation or dehumanization—an act of salvation. The artist is not only the mediator (Cazemajou*), the interpreter of tradition; he is the creator of new strategies. He may have a social or political role to play, not so much in offering resolutions as in suggesting ways to operate a synthesis, to overcome divisions. Certain writers emphatically call for a reuniting of the people, a reawakening and an end of frustration. Some have offered the possibility of escaping oppressive realistic or stereotypic representation, of finding a place of freedom and of expressing utopian longings.

One task set for the critic is to identify the ideology framed, consciously or not, in the work. This can be grasped through reconstruction of its lexical meaning or semantic system. In that perspective, literature is a socially symbolic act (Jameson, 1981), with an ideological utopian function, intent on finding imaginary solutions, salvational and redemptive to existing conflicts. The utopian formulation introduces new dynamics into the work, not only between the individual and the collective, but also between the reality of social life (the real as it is lived) and the way it is experienced imaginatively, metaphorically. The work thus expresses at the same time the social concreteness of which it is strikingly a part and a utopian resolution: a compensation for the pain endured and a way to secure a future. Utopia informs many works' structure: the figurative and highly eloquent language of Alurista's poetry as well as the more subdued prose of Anaya's "magical narratives", for example.

One is tempted here to draw attention to certain notions which have been presented in recent scholarship, that of the "political unconscious" (Jameson, 1981) and that of "art as a cultural system" (Geertz, 1983). Strategies of representation, we are told, do not so much depict the way things are in experience as the way they might be. What is given expression through art is the more suppressed, partially obscured or concealed facets of experience. Styles of feeling and states of mind, receiving a significant aesthetic form, assume a "truer" existence. Art helps shape and sustain them and generate a new distinctive sensibility, capable of eliciting the response of its audience. This theory of art in its relation to experience places the emphasis less on the mimetic, expressive character of art and more on the evocative, interactive. Artist, audience and aesthetic form are part of a larger collective experience which their mutual participation contributes to create.

In studying the process of literary construction—the building of the literary space—much attention has been given to the role of language and to the existence of intricate speech patterns that stem from the bilingual experience of most Hispanics. Through an interplay between Spanish and English—another symbolic act—linguistic devices have been created, which are considered to be a fundamental aspect of the poetics. Seizing upon the real, they transform and heighten it. Keller (in Jimenez, 1979, p. 263) has argued that those devices are not the mere reflection of actual speech patterns. Once they penetrate the literary work, they assume very precise and complex functions and interact with narrative registers, character representation, thematic and semantic organization. One of the reiterated principles of this poetics is the difference between the language of ordinary life and the literary work, between "word in life and word in poetry." The significance of bilingualism in literature is a source of much polemical debate. Speech patterns have been diversely designated as code switching, binary code system, expression of bisensitivity (Villanueva), interlinguality (Bruce-Novoa); blending two or more language systems, which may be harbored in the same voice (Nahualt, English, Spanish in Alurista's poetry), this interlinguality creates infinite possibilities which can be explored seriously or playfully. Each language comes from a particular experience, but their fusing and interaction are also part of the Hispanic linguistic culture. The result is an entirely new idiom, a second language system (Keller) and a deviation from normality and common language. Involved here are complex artistic techniques which assume parodic, metaphoric, empathic, hyperbolic, ritualistic or ceremonial functions. "Chicano" language itself offers a wide range of idioms—that of Vatos Locos, of Pachucos and campesinos, indigenous or modern, oral or written. Their integration in the literary text creates an infinite complexity of word play. New dynamics are at work, new combinations are being constantly devised between the diction and phonology, syntax and semantics, lexicon and morphology of each language. In the Paris conference Candelaria* and Aparicio* have studied these elaborate systems and suggested frames of interpretation for Chicano and Puerto Rican writing. Analyzing Nuyorican poetry, Aparicio has shown how the poetic manipulation of both languages receives many functions: to express the poet's stance toward the cultural values of North American and Puerto Rican life, to reaffirm Hispanicity or Hispanic indigenous realities, to fight against linguistic prejudice and regain vocality, to expand the possibilities of linguistic play and creativity.

The problem of readership of course arises at this point. Only the initiated reader will grasp the full significance of linguistic intricacies, and this secret coding may aggravate some of the problems with the publishing establishment or the difficulties of translation. The work itself may offer its own system of decoding, thus inducing new attitudes and reading practices. Each text in a sense evolves its own strategies and creates a unique new idiom. Each is definitely written with a precise audience in mind: Spanish or English-speaking or bilingual—and the issue of the basic language is still much debated. The advocates of a literature in Spanish envision beyond the Spanish-speaking community in the United States, a broader readership which includes Mexico, the islands, Latin America, Spain; those who propose English are oriented toward a totally different audience and market.

But whatever the language chosen, whatever the linguistic devices, imaginative and poetic manipulation may be, interplay between a multiplicity of dialects and idioms is seen as essential to the new poetics. It is through the coining of a new language that the artist transforms the raw materials of life, estranging the commonplace, challenging or undermining preexisting inherited conventions, transforming the readers' expectations and attitudes, their sense of space and time, their notion of events of characters.

Over the last three decades, the literary production has been impressive in the three main genres—fiction, poetry, drama—and marked by a great versatility. It has been accompanied by an equally important body of literary criticism and a wealth of ventures into more focused inquiries. The renaissance, "florecimiento" of the 1970's, to which many artists still express their attachment, has developed into a larger and sustained movement. Even though the dictates of El Movimiento may have forced the production into paths that are now judged as too narrow, the 1970's are still viewed as having created a determining breakthrough, as having given an unprecedented impetus to the artistic creativity. New generations are emerging, commanding attention, opening up new explorations. The critics have evinced a remarkable alertness, carrying on their investigations, spelling out priorities, reviewing and reevaluating the past and setting guidelines for the future. Crucial problems are still being addressed, mainly those which concern publication and readership. Hispanic literatures have definitely broadened their audiences and gained exposure through nationwide and in some cases international circulation. Recently more contacts have been made with the mainstream literary establishment. Yet the "ethnic" press and editors still have a major role to play in promoting these literatures and creating a reading public. The choice between several distribution networks, several potential audiences is the object of much controversy. The strategies which will be evolved have a crucial role to play in the construction of the poetics.

Through the intricate cultural matrix from which these literatures and art forms emerge, and through the interactive networks they have created, they present an entirely new profile whose complexity has still to be assessed. Although in its more recent stages, the production continues to assert itself as North American, it also overlaps and interpenetrates the Caribbean and Latin American spheres. Through its alternate use of English and Spanish, it is part of two equally impressive linguistic and literary empires. This interlinguality, the multi- and cross-cultural situation, with its constant spinning of new webs of significance, the openness to other cultures which is indispensable for a thorough understanding of its own, all account for the immense potentialities which are being offered: potentialities in the creative process and the elaboration of new canons, in the artistic exploration of infinite subtleties, in the recognition Hispanic art may eventually receive as it strives either for heightened symbolic closure or for more extended literary space.

In the Paris conference, the diversity and variety of art forms, the plurality of voices have been emphasized as well as the uniqueness of aesthetic forms. The papers offered a polyphone of interpretations of modes of reading, new interrogations and intuitions, and fresh insights. In the movement from theory to interpretation, most essays in this volume reveal the shape of both the literary and the critical Hispanic traditions, the nature of Hispanic poetics. Aspects that had been disputed or discredited have been reassessed, old premises reconsidered, new issues addressed in ways that were stimulating or provocative. New ideas and distinctions—innovative and challenging—have been presented. Most workshops and discussions have shown that it was possible to converse with one another across "the divide of cultural space." Without claiming to have reached a completely adequate and exhaustive understanding of Hispanic cultures, the analyses and interpretations offered have opened new paths toward the comprehension of art forms, to assess the claims they make on us and the kind of response they wish to elicit. Both the "mortal" and the "dialogic imagination" (Geerts, 1973; Bakhtin, 1981) have been constantly at work in order to fathom and construe the cultural uniqueness and the particular sensibility that these artistic forms convey and open out to us.

Bakhtin, M. *The Dialogic Imagination*, University of Texas Press, 1981.
Bruce-Novoa, J. "The Space in Chicano Literature," *De Colores*, 24, 1975. 22-4.
Cazemajou, J., ed. *Les minorités hispaniques en Amérique du Nord: échanges culturels et idéologiques*, Presses Universitaires de Bordeaux, 1985.
Flores, J. *Puerto-Rican Literature in the United States: Stages and Perspectives*.
Gates, H. L., ed. *Black Literature and Literary Theory*, Methuen, New York, 1984.
Geertz, C. *The Interpretation of Cultures*, New York Basic Books, 1973.
Gunn, G. *The Culture of Criticism and the Criticism of Culture*, Oxford University Press, 1987.
Harari, J. V. *Textual Strategies. Perspectives in Post Structural Criticism*, Cornell University Press, 1979.
Jameson, F. *The Political Unconscious*, Cornell University Press, 1981.
Jimenez, F., ed. *The Identification and Analysis of Chicano Literature*, Bilingual Press, 1979.
Leal, L. & Al, eds. *A Decade of Chicano Literature, 1970-1979*, Santa Barbara, CA 1982.
Mohr, E. *The Puerto Rican Experience*.
Ricoeur, P. *Interpretation Theory: Discourse and the Surplus of Meaning*, Texas Christian University Press, 1976.
Saldívar, R. "A Dialect of Difference," *Melus*, 63. Fall 1979, 73-92.
Shils, E. *Tradition*, University of Chicago Press, 1981.
Sommers, T. & Ybarra-Frausto, J., eds. *Modern Chicano Writers*, Prentice Hall, 1979.

Dissertations:

Clochez, C. *Les missions en Californie* (in progress). Grandjeat, C. Y. *La pruduction culturelle des Chicanos, 1960-1980* (unpublished).
Hasson, L. *L'image de la révolution cubaine dans la presse fruncaise et espugnole*, Editions hispaniques, Paris, 1980.
———. ed. *Cuba. Nouvelles et contes d'aujourd'hui*, L'Harmattan, Paris, 1985.
Lejeune, C. *La frontiere mexicano-américaine comme lieu de mémoire* (in progress)
Menendez, M. *L'homosexualité a Porto Rico et a New York* (unpublished).
Montel, A. *Travailleurs de la terre: images de l'ouvrier agricole au Colorado, 1965-1985* (in progress).
Rocard, M. *Les fils du soleil*, Maisonneuve el Larose, Paris, 1980.

"A midnight reality"[1]: Puerto Rican Poetry in New York, a Poetry of Dreams.

For Belén Fidalgo Colom

by Wolfgang Binder
Universität Erlangen

Any reader of Puerto Rican poetry written in New York City is bound to be struck by the frequency of the dream motif used in those works. Curiously enough, no publication has so far focused on this issue. This paper will, apart from an initial referal to Julia de Burgos and one other exception (José-Angel Figueroa), deal with poetry written in English by mainland Puerto Ricans. New York is, understandably, both its geographical and poetic center.

Already for the great Julia de Burgos (1914–1953) New York meant a highly ambiguous experience. Commenting on her first extended stay, which spanned from January to June, 1940, she wrote, overwhelmed by the modernity of the big city, to her sister Consuelo:

> [. . .] Aquí cada día abre nuevos horizontes y cada paso dado es una maravilla en el apretado haz de las sensaciones.
> [. . .] Imagínate nueve millones de habitantes en el radio de la ciudad. . . . Para todo este público tiene que haber tranvías y subways y trenes elevados, de manera que en cada esquina cambian de dirección y hay que ser experto en su telaraña.

She is unfavorably impressed by the architectural uniformity ("La ciudad en general [. . .] da la apariencia de un enorme cuartel militar[. . .]"), and shows a remarkable distance towards life in the *barrio*:

> Visité el otro día el Barrio Latino, donde se ven las más raras especies del género humano. Todos esos tipos grotescos de las películas se ven caminando por Nueva York. [. . .]

A few days before the above quoted impressions, on January 25, 1940, Julia wrote to Consuelo:

> Estoy casi desconcertada en este país. Mucho más que ahora, en los primeros días. Hubo instantes en que quería volver de aquí a cualquier sitio más sereno y hospitalario [. . . .] No es tanto la terrible realidad de un frío que hiela los huesos, y de una perspectiva de máquina y rutina, sino la gigantesca ola de esfuerzos y contratiempos que traje en mi cerebro desde esa tierra, tan dura de justicia[. . .]²

This passage of *destierro* is important since it reminds us of the fundamental subjectivity of each commentator and of the equally relevant fact that each migrant, emigrant or visitor (poet or not) carries with him or herself a heavy cargo of cultural, socio-political and quite personal emotional items.

For Julia de Burgos this implied a deeply tragic love life coupled with an astute political awareness about the colonial status of her country. In the posthumously published volume *El mar y tú* (1954) texts appear that exude solitude, desperation, and continuing deaths and now New York becomes a territory of broken dreams:

> ¡Corre, que se muere
> que se muere le sueño!³

New York's urban stone structures are turned into metaphors for lack of affection, for isolation and a yearning for unrequited love as in "Media tarde":

> Media tarde
> sollozos de piedra y de cauces
> remotos a mi alrededor.
>
> Media tarde
> Nueva York, contemplaba tu
> feria de verano[. . .]⁴

Whereas Julia de Burgos' use of New York as a dream space is above all a privatistic one, Puerto Rican poets writing and living in that city since the sixties have repeatedly extended this aspect and produced collective dreams and visions that are based on a common socio-cultural and economic reality.

In Pedro Pietri's "Puerto Rican Obituary" six characters representing the Puerto Rican community on the mainland die dreaming false dreams (e.g. being part of a "clean-cut lily-white neighborhood", or "about the ideal/ white american/ family/ with black maids").⁵ Eager acceptance of a white middle-class American Way of Life is for the poet a dissolution of a multiracial Caribbean identity and ultimately death. In his poem "The Broken English Dream," Pietri paints another fresco of slum life peopled by exploited and self-deluded inhabitants. In his bitter resumé he states:

> [. . .]
> To the united states we came
> To learn how to mispell [sic] our name
> To lose the definition of pride
> To have misfortune on our side
> To live where rats and roaches roam
> in a house that is definitely not a home
> To be trained to turn on television sets
> To dream about jobs you will never get
> [. . . .]⁶

In the same category of protest poetry interspersed with surreal images belongs José-Angel Figueroa's "A Conversation w/ Coca Cola." Here, too, the poet functions as spokesman for a group; a note of didacticism is inevitable. Dreams turn into nightmares in the context of economic exploitation:

> [. . .] latin souls wake up
> like swollen dreams in the middle of the night
> ever since con edison raised the rent
> and the landlords executed the hot water
> [. . . .]⁷

Jesús Pappoleto Meléndez joins Pietri and Figueroa (with whom he formed, in the seventies, a mock gang) in his early poem "have you seen liberation," as he strikes both the protest and the didactic note:

> [. . .]
> have you seen the Puerto Ricans/
> nodding on the stoops/
>   their heads bowed down
>   in a shameless dream.
>
> have you seen the Puerto Ricans/
> in el barrio/ south bronx/ new york

> america/
>> running down the street
>> chasing their own sisters & brothers
>> & stealing from them
>> to buy a bag of futile dreams.
> [. . . .]⁸

The military voice at the end of the poem gave way to a milder voice in his second, and, so far, last volume, *Street Poetry & Other Poems* (1972). Here he perceives contents of garbage cans, refuse Americana, as objects of affection and attention for Puerto Rican children in New York:

> [. . .]
> Garbage cans/ sitting in lonely sidewalks
> filled to the brim with used dreams
> [. . .]
> children passing
> as slow as life moves itself
>> stopping/ searching
>> & finding dreams in those garbage cans/
>> taking them home & playing with them.⁹

Two poems of the same collection by Meléndez mention dreams in connection with drug addicts. In "the loneliest of loneliness" the speaker shares a pessimistic vision with the reader after he "tripped over a straw & entered a dream":

> [. . .]
> the visions began:
>> rain rained on a rainy day/ clouds congregated
>> then peed into the Piss-pot of life
> forming tiny lakes on the cracks of ghetto sidewalks/
> forming rivers of ghetto gutters/ flooding sewers.
> in the rivers bums laid singing/
> "old man river"
> while their off-key lyrics drowned in the sewers/
>> as all my lonely dreams.
> [. . . .]

In this world of ugliness and death the connection between the first person speaker and the group of drug addicts is established towards the end of the text:

> [. . .]
> i went to a party
> the junkies used the bathrooms as a shooting gallery/
> they tripped/ over mistakes & entered dreams
> /heard people laughing tears
> tears which they tasted and found to be bitter
> [. . .]
> & in their dreams they saw me
> tripping/ over a straw & entering dreams.[10]

Meléndez' poem "spring again" fuses the sense if timelessness ("a long wait/ a slow wait") with the concept of seasons. In a universe devoid of love, filled with monotony—even the games youngsters enjoy are depicted as endless repetitions—dreams abound:

> [. . .]
> & dreams escape
> & become stolen & lost & used
> & wasted & thrown away
> & dreamed again
>
> the junkies sit on the stoop
> & nod themselves into dreams
> /maybe into the ones which escaped/
> [. . . .][11]

Miguel Piñero, whose drama output is more widely known than his poetry, has a poem which gives vent to the speaker's visions of greatness, of (illusionary) eminence, of the status of a community spokesman of Superman proportions. The yearning is, evidently, an expression of the lack of power and glory:

> dreamt i was a poet
> &
> writin' silver sailin' songs
> words
> strong & powerful crashing thru
> walls of steel & concrete
> erected in minds weak
> [. . .]
> i dreamt i was this poetry
> words glitterin' brite & bold
> strikin' a new rush for gold
> in las bodegas

where our poets' words & songs
   are sung
   [. . . .]

The illusion of the dream is broken by the advent of daylight:

   but
   sunlite stealin' thru venetian
   blinds
   eyes hatin', workin' of time
   [. . . .]
   poets' [sic] dreams
   endin' in a factoria as one
   in a million
   unseen
   [. . . .][12]

In 1980 Sandra María Esteves, a poet, painter and actress living in the South Bronx, published a book of poems entitled *Yerba Buena*. It contains three variants of the dream motif. A feminist one tied up with a call to freedom make "A Julia y a Mí" a liberating text on more than one level. The poem is aptly dedicated to Julia de Burgos. Esteves identifies with Julia's emotional suffering, yet affirms her Afro-Caribbean womanly life force:

   [. . .]
   women still tend fires that men burn
   and lovers still imprison dreams
   and truth remains cold like your bones yet bittersweet
   [. . . .]
   my fist is my soul
   it cuts into the blood of dragons
   and marks time with the beat
   of an afrocuban drum.[13]

One of the recurring motifs in New York based Puerto Rican literature is the Edenic vision of the island.[14] Esteves, who has never lived in Puerto Rico, uses the topos of the mythic *locus amoenus* in an exchange between reality and dream. An imagined past becomes a psycho-cultural reality that serves as an identity marker:

   [. . .]
   I may never overcome
   the theft of my isla heritage

> dulces palmas de coco on Luquillo
> sway in windy recesses I can only imagine
> and remember how it was
>
> But that reality now a dream
> teaches me to see, and will
> bring me back to me.[15]

In "For South Bronx" she starts out with a stark depiction of housing conditions of that area:

> I live amidst hills of desolate buildings
> rows of despair
> crowded together
> in a chain of lifeless shells
> [. . . .]

Her poem ends with an illusion to the colorful grafitti sprayed on the subway trains in their Bronx terminal. These orgies of color and movement she interprets as visual appeals, as expressions of stifled lives:

> [. . .]
> the youngbloods invade the trainyards
> laden with colors of dreams
> crying for existence
> [. . . .][16]

A conciliatory if lucid position is taken by the Black Puerto Rican poet and playwright Tato Laviera in his latest book, *AmeRícan*. In the title poem he perceives the New York Puerto Rican has a blend of Caribbean and mainland traits, as an integrating and harmonizing force. Laviera's dream is thrusting itself forward into the future and has a utopian dimension in a free, truly multicultural United States:

> [. . .]
> AmeRícan, yes, for now, for i love this, my second
>   land, and i dream to take the accent from
> the altercation, and be proud to call
>   myself american, in the U.S. sense of the
>   word, AmeRícan, America![17]

The most fertile poet as far as the dream motif is concerned we find to be Victor Hernández Cruz. In his work dreams range from the most banal literal usage (as in "After Dancing")[18] to collective cultural manifestations in music, to apocalyptic visions and double reality. Like Miguel Algarín,[19] he sees one of the great *salseros*, Ray Barretto, as an identity enhancing force who with increasing signs of ecstasy takes possession of an ethnic group and an area of greater New York:

> [. . .]
> it was you
> [. . .]
> coming at me
> with your drums/ you
> soul drummer you who went
> away
> [. . .]
> your fingers bleeding
> bleeding your eyes closed
> [. . .]
> the bronx is ours the bronx
> take the bronx & shhhhhit
> listen
> the dance the dance
> o the stairs o the window
> will be broken [. . . .]

The underlying orality of the text, a phenomenon encountered so often in New York Puerto Rican poetry, is able to carry the rhythmic adhesion to salsa music and to heighten the mystical trance-like qualities which remind the reader of *santería* rituals:

> [. . .]
> sleep sleep sleep
> down down down
> softly
> the piano plays our memories
> our dreams our loves [. . .]
> You already there
> nothing stopping you
> you are magic
> magic
> magic
> espíritu libre
> espíritu libre
> [. . . .][20]

Snaps, by the same author contains also an apocalyptic fire storm in "urban dream." Scenes of utter destruction ("times square/ electrified, burned, smashed, stomped"), are followed by human dismemberment mingled with surreal details:

> [. . .] bones & ashes, all over
> blood & broken lips that their head somewhere else, all
>   over
> livers & bright white skulls with hair on them, standing
>   over a river
> watching hamburgers floating by. Steaks with teeth in
>   them.
> flags & chairs & beds & golf sets & mickey mouse broken
>   in half.
> [. . . .]

In the third section of the poem, ongoing breathless disintegration of land and humans finds itself accompanied by pop music —"the brothers five sing the blues as they sink."(118) The ending consists of a cryptic statement which hints both at a loss of orientation and new, archaic faiths:

> & someone sings & someone laughs [sic] & nobody knows.
> & chant to gods.
> & chant to gods.[21]

Victor Hernández Cruz included in his second book, *Mainland*, published in 1973 by Random House, several poems that take up the dream motif. In one of the most successful, "Thursday," a rainy Manhattan assumes through the filter of recollection a liquidity which is associated with the sea and a tropical island. Thursday also becomes personified in a much loved woman, in music and the Spanish tongue:

> Water is Manhattan
> The trains and the buses they sail
> Stores and the lights
> In the water wet
> Thursday far and near strange
> A dream Thursday and island
> There are two in the memory.

A creolization of New York becomes immersed in the admittedly unreal tropical (Puerto Rican) idyl and the possibility of a love:

> [. . .]
> Today I eat guineo

> With my hands
> Under a palm tree by the beach
> Where I am not
> Do you see the dance that could begin
> Evolve.(8f)

This double reality—removed, in addition, by an act of recollection—seems to correspond to the ill-defined state of acculturation of many Puerto Ricans in New York. It surfaces in "Side 8," a poem written in a humorous vein, in Hernández Cruz' *Tropicalization* (1976). Life in New York as a whole is grasped in its unreal, illusionary essence and put into a structure resembling the *bolita*, the illegal numbers game, and a litany derived from spiritualist and *santería* practices as well as children's games:

> This town is the numbers game
> Each morning we decipher our dreams
> In front of 7 put 11
> A pregnant woman but no nightmare
> In front of 2 put 10
> A relative that came in unexpectant
> Around the 8 add 16
> [. . . .]
> Dreaming with a wedding definite hit
> Seven book says 610
> Seven o'clock in the evening
> The horses come home
> We shit on 10.[22]

As we have seen, the dream motif and images related to it have served militant protest and engaged poetry (Pietri, Figueroa, Meléndez), hypertrophied personal aspirations (Piñero), poetry of a feminist persuasion (Esteves), a poetry of appeal (Esteves, also all poets listed in our first category), a poetry of apocalyptic dimensions (Hernández Cruz), a poetry of utopian harmony for the mainland Puerto Rican (Laviera), and a poetry of creolization (Hernández Cruz). The inherent instability of dreams, their fragility, but also the wide range of possible experiences on "real" and "unreal" levels offered a host of stratagems to poets of a group and culture which are menaced by assimilation and exploitation.

¹From Jesús Papoleto Meléndez, *have you seen liberation* (No place, no publication, 1969), 19. I refrain from using the terms "Nuyorican" or "neorrican" in this text since by no means all of the poets mentioned would be happy with it. Spelling, spaces and punctuation of the quotes correspond to the originals.
²All quotes are from Yvette Jiménez de Báez, *Julia de Burgos. Vida y poesía* (San Juan: Editorial Coquí, 1966), 30ff. No complete biography of the poet exists as yet, nor has her family released her papers in their totality.
³"Naufragio de un sueño," in *El mar y tú. Otros poemas* (Río Piedras: Ediciones Huracán, 1981), 49.
⁴"Media tarde," *El mar*, 74f.
⁵*Puerto Rican Obituary* (New York—London: Monthly Review Press, 1973), 1-12.
⁶*Ibid.*, 13.
⁷In *East 110th Street* (Detroit: Broadside Press, 1973), 15.
⁸See footnote No. 1; here 20.
⁹Published by Barlemir House, New York, 46.
¹⁰*Ibid.*, 47.
¹¹*Ibid.*, 50f.
¹²*La Bodega Sold Dreams* (Houston: Arte Público Press, 1980), 5f. See also Piñero's "cheap/F.M./dreams" and "wino dreams" in his "New York City Hard Times Blues," in the same collection, 42, 47.
¹³*Yerba Buena*. Greenfield Review Chapbook 47 (Greenfield Center, New York: Greenfield Review, 1980), 50f.
¹⁴See Wolfgang Binder, "Die Nordwanderung der Puertoricaner und ihre Literatur," in Berndt Ostendorf, ed. *Amerikanische Gettoliteratur. Zur Literatur ethnischer, marginaler und unterdückter Gruppen in Amerika*. Impulse der Forschung 42 (Darmstadt: Wissenschaftliche Buchgesllschaft, 1983), 323-55; Efraín Barradas, " 'De lejos en sueños verla. . . ' visión mítica de Puerto Rico en la poesía neorrican," *Revista Chicano-Riqueña* 8, No.4 (1979), 46-56.
¹⁵S. Esteves, *Yerba*, 20.
¹⁶*Ibid.*, 84.
¹⁷Published by Arte Público Press, Houston, 1985: 95.
¹⁸*Snaps* (New York: Random House, 1969), 49.
¹⁹See his poem of homage, "Ray Barretto: December 4, 1976," in *On Call* (Houston: Arte Público Press, 1980), 14f.: "Barretto maestro,/ Barretto, maestro to futuristic people/ who have wakeful dreams for breakfast/ [. . .] Barretto, Doctor of Body Motion,/ you release the monster that chews/ the working man from inside out,/ la gente se menea con tu ritmo [. . .].
²⁰*Ibid.*, 71 ff.
²¹*Ibid.*, 117f.
²²Published by Reed, Cannon & Johnson Communications Co., no place; 20.

Ricardo Sánchez: The Poetics of Liberation

by Yves-Charles Grandjeat
University of Bordeaux

As the foremost representative of "pinto" poetry, Sánchez, whose first published poems were written in jail, and who spent more than seven years in various California and Texas institutions, epitomizes the condition of a Chicano caught in a hostile society. Thus, he has probably been able to assess, better than anyone else, the liberating power of language. A study of his poetry may therefore provide us with some clues helping us to understand the specific power and function of literary production in the context of the Chicano movement. Now, a cursive look at Sánchez's writings between 1961 and 1979 shows a striking evolution in his tone and mood, from the feeling of anger and protest pervading the volume *Canto y Grito mi Liberación*[1] published in 1971, to the 1976 volume entitled *Hechizospells*[2], on to the 1981 booklet *Brown Bear Honey Madness*[3] where the poet, at one with the world and himself, seems to have reached a sense of fulfilled self-realization. Eighteen years of living but also of writing appear to have brought him from panic to peace, from separation to synthesis. In his late writings, we find the mature poet, quietly revelling in life, blissfully wedded to each passing memory or sensation, wading in love. A Chicano Walt Whitman, he roams the universe, happily taking stock of reality's ever-changing and multiple facets and merging each fragment into the whole:

> I walk you, America
>   north to south,
>   east to west
> all of you,
>   a beautiful woman
>   of a land. . . .
> I bathe in your experiences,
> celebrate
>   whatever possible
> you are so many
>   just as I am
>   so many me's (BB 31-33)

It has been a long, twisted way to this statement of serene merging with the world. For Sánchez's early writings, as a contrast, clearly rise from a gap, a yearning, a fearful feeling of isolation, the terrible sense of frustration with the world which made him first slip into lawlessness. Ironically, the prison then became a concrete metaphor for his innermost feelings. Indeed, the two poems by Sánchez which open *Canto y Grito mi Liberación* hinge on the two key words of "separation" and "solitude." The first one bears no title and opens with a nostalgic vision fraught with feelings of loss, pain and estrangement. Another key word in this opening poem is "busco," which clearly defines writing as a quest, a search for something lost:

> vi la lluvia anoche, amor mío
> sentí el duelo
> y nos separemos
> hoy te busco
> en los callejones
> de mi mente/alma (CG 17)

The volume significantly continues with the poem "Soledad," where the actual jail blends with a "mind jail," haunted by similar feelings of loss, obsessive, relentless loneliness and maddening nostalgia:

> soledad
>   my soul bleats
> lonely, lonely, lonely
> a night—some time ago
> long ago—Los Panchos
> sang of
>   women of perdition
> and love. (CG 27)

Women, love and loss are here intimately associated. In *Hechizospells*, the poem "Toward" beautifully conveys the plight of the poet, forever laboring to recapture through his words the ghost of a by-gone mental and physical plenitude, the shadow of a paradise lost:

> toward, toward, ever toward
> that infernal struggle to present
> all the awesome realities of being
> lost
> in being lost . . .
> and only thoughts

> roam
> lean streets
> searching for
> a once had/now lost
> sustenance
> I am
> a shadow of my thoughts
> I am
> a groping towards light. (H 184)

It is worth following Sánchez's path toward the "liberation of a Chicano mind" which he announces in his first volume of poetry. It is my contention that his poetry, both through the structure of its imagery and through the linguistic texture of its fabric, not only reflects this process, but also activates it, helping the writer complete his "trip through the mind jail" and out of it. Sánchez, like others of his fellow poets—Alurista, for instance—explicitly wages a psychological battle against fear and conflict on three complementary levels: the physical senses through sound and rhythm, the explicitly symbolic using clear metaphors, and implicitly symbolic, devising linguistic constructs which themselves become metaphors for actual life processes. Thus the text is perceived as a physical medium, a reservoir of metaphors, and a linguistic process endowed with with mimetic power. Chicano poets have made outstanding inroads on this last level due to their exceptional historical, social, cultural and linguistic position. Moreover, someone like Sánchez combines on a personal level a wide array of experiences, from pachuco rebel and "pinto" poet to professor; he can freely run a wide gamut of representations and linguistic registers. But it is on all three levels—physical, metaphorical, and linguistic—that the poet strives to achieve his double goal: energizing and synthesizing, exorcising fear and death, and bridging the gap between once mutually exclusive elements.

Sánchez's first words are, first and foremost, sounds. AYYYYY-YYYYY!, he shouts in poems which are often written to be read out loud and strike the senses with physical forcefulness. They edge on pure emotion, which they are meant both to convey and unleash. Sánchez's "grito," echoing Ginsberg's howl, first rings with pain, protest and anger. Writing, like shouting, is a means of summoning up essential life forces in the midst of a desperate struggle against death, while providing an antidote to dementia for this "stowaway on the last boat to insanity" (CG 86), offering a vital outlet to rage:

> —and it hurts, and it hurts, andithurts

>   hasta que mi misma casta
>   GRITA
>   a ringing obscenity even more obscene. . . ! (CG 40)

Howls of pain are mixed with shouts of hate. The "grito" then develops into a threat and an indictment, a weapon hurled at the enemy, daring him to the fight: "Our chests now swell with anger and every gringo, CADA UNO DE ESOS PINCHES GRINGOS—is a target" (CG 36). It becomes a ritualistic cry of war, emphasized by the frequent use of capital letters:

>   ubicando mi mente
>   es el grito de
>   GRINGOS MATENLOS (CG 82)

But "gritos," for Sánchez, are not just aimed at the enemy, or intended for himself, as a release: they are also directed at the Chicano or other reader or listener, to sting, stab, jolt him out of his lethargy, rouse him from the "slow, sickening death" creeping over him and trigger him into action. For Sánchez, excess is both a need and a method aimed at stirring up energy through a sort of mimesis: it must provoke what it evokes. Indeed, when he does not shout, Sánchez rants and raves without restraint. Emotion then is not conveyed by the intensity of each line, but by the collective momentum of words rushing in wild sequences, as when he indicts America: "genocidically manic nation," "mad-dog society," "land of public liberty," "from the heinous perversity of Manhattan to the sordidness of the South, from the infested sores and hunger of Appalachia to the mafiosi hideousness of Chicago, and from the putrid avariciousness of the Texas tragic valley to the sophisticated hypocrisy of California" (CG 31) or the American way of life, this "regimented idiocy," "alien form of cretinism," etc. Here, of course, one also senses a drastic reversal of dominant value. The culprit becomes the prosecutor. But the sheer power of utterance is as effective a weapon, in this struggle, as the notions conveyed.

The poet obviously wastes no time lashing out at one enemy already reeling from self-inflicted blows and seemingly headed for a fall. Rather, he uses his words as spurs, to instill life energy into the reader. Shouting and ranting are two basic means of loading language with sheer emotion and vitality. Strong rhythmic patterns also contribute to impart the text with physical forcefulness, and Sánchez makes skillful use of sound effects, tempo, alliteration and assonance as, for instance, in the beautiful poem "Viento, history and drum" (H 205-214), where words echo like "the rolling thunder/of drums of matachines/. . . on the/flaps of wind/

howling through our minds," touching off a sort of anamnesis:

> I remember words
> of drum—drum of my people—
> chicano drum, / indigeno drum
> beating out sounds. . . .
> with furious beat and ritmo
>   ca-tum-ba, ca-tum-ba,
>   tun-tun-pa,
>   ca-tum-ba, ca-tum-ba,
>   tun-tun-pa,
>   ca-tum-ba, cat-tum-ba,
>   tun-tun-pa. . . .

Sounds and beat, through the physical energy they convey, succeed in revitalizing the mind. For, although physical domination is unacceptable: "Chicanitos born only to die/swollen eyes and bellies/in the land of plenty" (CG 40), mental oppression is a much more subtle and effective means to subject the victim. For Sánchez, and this is where the power of the poet is most called for, the struggle must be primarily fought and won in the mind, those "mind-souls polluted/with vicious images/of our subservience" (H 9), where words are endowed with the ability to unleash or stifle desire, give faith or crush hope, induce or hinder action. This is clearly what Sánchez means when he writes that

> words which sound
> trite, overused, abused
> beget tired actions
> and wilted sensation (. . .)
> clinches—for some—are better
> than expletives or explosions. . . . (BB 30)

His own expletives or explosions zero in on crippling images of the enemy's power, while heating up, to fever pitch, whatever creative energy might slumber in the reader's mind.

Metaphors, in this regard, are another means for the poet to achieve effectiveness. The love and sex imagery, especially, which pervades Sánchez's writings enable him further to whip up and celebrate vital energy. Sexual energy represents raw, unfettered vitality brought to a climax, while sexual encounters provide a model for what a fulfilled existence could and should be. In an early text, as he recalls his sexual initiation with a Juarez prostitute, Sánchez clearly shows sexual experience as the gateway to manhood. Coming of age implies becoming sexually active and, accordingly, being a man required remaining sexually alert. And Sánchez does, dream-thoughts constantly on the prowl, eyes on the rove, always ready to snatch some sweet erotic hint from the midst of some serious "bureaucratic meeting":

> Piernas llenas de riqueza mestiza
> she caught me
> smiling/looking avidly
> and graciously shifted
> so that skirt rode up just enough
> to bless my fevered/thirsting eyes
> with a massaging gobbling sight
> of her lacey woman's bounty (H 161)

Sex, however, is sometimes associated with painful connotations and Sánchez uses it both as a positive and a negative metaphor. It can evoke feelings of destruction "Resonating hurt/ deracinating selfness/ spent like a used condom" (CG 85). Although in most cases sexuality takes on such connotations when Sánchez indicts what he sees as the sick cocktail of Anglo puritanism and debauchery, gloomy undertones slip here and there into his writings:

> "Like all women
> you were born to die
> and dying shall leave you
> dessicated
> devoid of soul
>   too soon" (CG 47)

One senses here a double-edged attitude towards sex, and indeed, sexuality is where ambivalence is simultaneously stated and resolved: "two big thighs one brown, one black/ engulf/ and swallow up/ resolve. . . " (CG 67). It is a realm where the dialectics of duality and unity are constantly at work, each merging into the other. Moreover, when enjoyed in the context of marriage, where it can develop into mother and fatherhood, sex becomes even more closely identified with vitality and synthesis. Thus, the sex, love and family imagery are paramount insofar as it associates the two key functions in Sánchez's poetry: energizing and integrating. For loving brings about the linking of the self with the other, of the many into the one:

> "Loins/souls pulse
> in rhythm

> with mind
> within the universe of love shared
> as another linking moment
> in time's continuum
> is caressed." (H 169)

Indeed, linkage is at the core of Sánchez's poetry: vitality is to be shared, whether on a personal or on a broader social level: "It is through sharing that we will create a moral world, mutuality is the key" (CG 16). The family, in this regard is a choice metaphor: as a cluster of love in which each individual accepts, respects and loves the other in both a physical and sentimental way, it provides a microcosm of what an ideal society should be. The family is the living proof that life and creation spring from a combination of diversity and sharing:

> "In the midst of our pobreza,
> we bask in each other's arms (. . .)
> you murmur of creation
> as our beings fuse in love
> and your being glows aborning
> our next child's loved gestation."

Writing, for Sánchez, is clearly meant to materialize into a medium. While interaction runs as a theme through the poems' imagery, it is also ceaselessly practiced in the act of writing, which primarily comes across as a mediating process, as evidenced by the linguistic fabric woven by the poet, who deliberately mixes an amazing variety of registers. Code-switching from English to Spanish is doubled by what we might venture to call stylistic code-switching, combining sophisticated, learned phrasing rife with esoteric or even foreign expressions, with bits and pieces sometimes crude language, while constantly wavering between extremely abstract and forcefully physical utterance. Such linguistic interaction and synthesis clearly takes on a metaphorical value: for finding a language of liberation clearly implies achieving the liberation of language. As Sánchez writes: "Cal" is as valid, if not more so, as grammatical English and/or Spanish. To feel put down because we have created new linguistic dimensions to life is idiocy, for human interactions have always affected language" (H 20). Similarly, we may argue that constant linguistic interaction and metamorphosis affirm the possibility and necessity of human cross-pollination. Thus, throughout the whole volume of *Canto y Grito*, Sánchez keeps bursting through any limitation imposed by set codes, blending prose with poetry, reaching for an integrated form. In

"Existir es" (CG 145-153), for instance, he intersperses personal recollections with lyrics from what he calls "a few songs from the barrio" written in the classical "corrido" form. Elsewhere, he alternates classical poetry written in formal meter and rhyme with free verse. Sánchez is probably at his best when he uses expressive everyday language from the barrio, as he does in "Batos de los" (H 74):

"que lucas, ese,
that like in high school,
here in la pinta,
we make appointments
to get in on
some buey-ese,
if we were in el chuco
you don't ask a bato
for chingazos,
you just go
for what you know
to be the way to go."

His writing then flows fluently, endowed with maximum suggestiveness and rich tempo where physical expressiveness is greatly enhanced by a skillful use of alliteration and assonace, as well as rhythmic patterns and disruptions:

"and it churns,
on and on,
my being burns. . .
hung by balls,
hurt by hate,

However, Sánchez simultaneously displays a jarring taste for abstract, complicated wording which often mars his poetic effectiveness. Lines such as

community burgeoning into
    power acknowledgement is
fastly relegated
    to bureaucratic consignment
to meaningless coffers
    in great social structures (H 85)

smack of what he himself has labeled "trite passionless clichéd outburst" and evidence a marked propensity to indulge in bombastic phrasing. His liability to use philosophical abstractions in his love poems, stultifying emotions, turning them into intellectualized statements, or blunting them with complicated wording is at first quite disturbing. Actually, *Canto y Grito* literally swarms with abstractions. A quick survey would reveal an astounding wealth of "tion" suffixes, such as, to mention but a few,

> condemnation, retribution, tintinnabulation, laceration, precipitation, musication, salivation, attenuation, equation, rejection, refraction, cremation, fulmination, attribution, deprivation, destitution, machination, genuflection, dementation, absolution, ablution, etc.

Sánchez's vocabulary is so fraught with abstract and even foreign words that it often borders on the esoteric. We find the Latin particle "cum" the French "esprit," "jour," "vis-a-vis," the German "angst" and "verboten," etc. In fact, the poet seems ruled by an urge to expand, explode and explore the lexicon available to him, trying out words, coining others, delighting in sheer linguistic experimentation and accumulation. In a poem such as "A.M. Bleakness" (H 102), words seems to run amuck into a caricature of abstract poetry but then, as the poem unravels, Sánchez eases back into expressive, physical language impulsed by powerful tempo. His deliberate aim then seems to bring opposite registers to clash into unexpected combinations, constantly taking us off-guard and sending us off-balance:

> all feel lonely
> even the wispy kids
> hustling
> tired old men
> within palaced arcades (. . .)
>
> quickie-quickie, chop-chop
> and some do plop and lop
> venereal surcease
> white/black/yellow/red/brown/orificity
> mechanized with much simplicity (. . .) (H 103)

The words "venereal surcease" and "orificity" for instance disrupt the rhythm that had been set, and keep us from settling into a pattern.

The poet, in fact, achieves a writing based on perpetual interaction, weaving together a startling, highly baroque lingusitic fabric, addressing in turn the intellect and the senses, carrying out in the text a perfect, compelling mimesis of what humanity should really be about:

> black, brown,
> white, red
> yellow and mestizo,
>
> all in the human process
> evolving out of muck,
>
> turbulent, hating, hurting
> mankind on the rampage... (CG 159)

Sánchez's poems illustrate how writing, both as a medium and as a mediating process, can fulfill a therapeutic function. Poetry may stand out as the form most likely to accommodate the writer's teeming, urgent emotions. It can help overcome the sense of alienation, or, to quote Chicano poet and critic Rafael Gonzales, of "cultural dislocation"[5] which has plagued Chicanos exposed to the material and cultural domination of an Anglo environment, providing a vital response to threats of mental wreckage. As the genre closest to the Mexican-American popular oral tradition, with poems often written to be read in public, it made possible what Tomás Ybarra-Frausto has termed "the recovery of a voice." For Ybarra, the surge of Chicano poetry reflected a process of social change: "For the campesino, the passage from serf to self liberated the imagination and made possible the recovery of a voice."[6] But the process also works the other way around. The power of language should not be underrated: the recovery of a voice makes equally possible the passage from serf to self. Sánchez's itinerary evidences how images and actions, fiction and fact intertwine in a dialectical process of mental and social change. Indeed, when conflict is integrated and tackled within the texture of the text, language restructures reality not only vicariously, but also in actuality, insofar as it can alter one's perception of it, including the perception of one's power to act upon it. To this extent, each Chicano writer uses literature, in Alurista's words, "not only as a reflective art but as a healing art, a surgical tool."[7] Sánchez acts in no other way when he symbolically releases boiling, potentially lethal emotions and trashes the enemy with his words. Then after galvanizing the self, he reconciles it with the world, making use of mediating symbols and integrating a multifaceted experience into a creative pattern, weaving together once mutually exclusive words, registers, images and mental schemes into the bold fabric of his poems. In the process, while travelling from protest to praise, he contributes, like most Hispanic writers have, to push back a little further the limits of American literature.

[1] Ricardo Sánchez, *Canto y Grito mi Liberación*, (New York: Anchor Books, 1973.)
[2] *HechizoSpells*, Los Angeles: UCLA Chicano Studies Center Publications, 1976.
[3] *Brown Bear, Honey Madness*, (Austin: Slough Press, 1981.)
[4] All quotations from Ricardo Sánchez's poems will be referred to according to the following code:
BB 31-33: *Brown Bear, Honey Madness*, pp. 31-33.
CG 17: *Canto y Grito mi Liberación*, p. 17.
H 184: *Hehcizospells*, p. 184.
[5] "Chicano Poetry/Smoking Mirror", in *New Directions in Chicano Scholarship*, Ricardo Romo & Raymund Paredes eds. (Santa Barbara: University of California-Santa Barbara Center for Chicano Studies Monographs, 1984), p. 95.
[6] "The Chicano Movement and the emergence of a Chicano Poetic Consciousness," in *New Directions for Chicano Studies*, op.cit.
[7] In Juan Bruce-Novoa, *Chicano Authors, Inquiry by Interview*, (Austin: University of Texas Press, 1980), p. 280.

The Recovery of Nineteenth Century Chicano Autobiography

by Genaro Padilla
University of California-Berkeley

I

Although autobiography study is flourishing, almost nothing has been written about the autobiographical tradition in Chicano culture.[1] One would think that there has been no autobiographical voice within a culture that has had a vital literary tradition for hundreds of years. It is as though individual Chicanos had not marked their lives to paper, had lived and then disappeared from history without a trace. This is partly true, but certainly not because of illiteracy or disinclination. Chicanos have been silenced not only by the grave, but by social transformation, linguistic alienation, political narratives that seal life history into textual permanence. Memoirs so long out of print they have nearly forgotten themselves. Diaries, family histories, personal poetry, collections of self-disclosing correspondence. Much more autobiographical material unpublished and, although catalogued, forgotten on archive shelves. Lives scattered on broken pages, faded, partially lost at the margins, suspended in language unuttered until there is a listener who opens the file and begins. The archeological project to recover Chicano autobiography thus begins here.

The primary requirement of such an archaeological project might appear to be only that of digging through archives in search of material that will reconstitute the autobiographical tradition in Chicano culture. Indeed, identifying and recovering autobiographical material is a major undertaking, especially when such work has no precedent. Once the recovery is in process, however, there appears an entire set of considerations that must be decided upon before working through the first box of aging papers. It means deciding upon the kind of material I choose to define as autobiographical, a theoretical issue that rests on current debate over the definition of what constitutes "true" autobiography. It means deciding at which point in history I choose to intervene. And it means defining the ideological prerogatives that determine which material I choose to collect, examine, and comment upon. It means, ultimately, deciding upon the ideology of my own interpretive stance, especially since I am in a position, at least for the moment, to recover those autobiographical texts that reaffirm my own ideological purpose, while allowing certain texts to remain silenced because their politics does not coincide with mine.

On the issue of what kind of texts constitutes an autobiography, I at once expand the classic definition of autobiography as a sustained "I" conscious prose narrative in which the individual author is consumed in the act of recreating the history of the "self", with particular emphasis on the internal life and the development of his or her personality.[2] I wish to broaden the definition of autobiography to include the contextualized "I," the relation of the history of the "I" as an adjunct to the relation of an external historical matrix, the relative displacement of an "I" centered text by a "We" configuration. For example, I want to include texts that many scholars would consider more properly within the domain of "history," but which I believe an autobiographical reading will discover to be Autobiography as much as History. I admit to reading for autobiographical intent and content, but do so in the belief that the individuals who composed or related communal histories were simultaneously composing the history of the self and its shaping, twisting, reconfigurating response to social transformation.

While I do not wish to privilege one form over another, I do believe that my part in the recovery of Chicano autobiography is currently in a stage that requires constraints on the inclusion of types and genres of material—rather than being a problem, however, this is cause for celebration since it issues from the wealth and multiplicity of autobiographic material that is recoverable. Therefore, although diaries, bodies of correspondence, personal lyrics, and many *corridos*/ballads, for example, impress me as autobiographic documents, I have made the decision, both arbitrary and provisional for now, to discuss only prose narratives. In the case of some of the material, the length of the text is such that I use the term "episodic" to describe narratives that are brief (some only 15 to 20 pages) and often focus only upon a contained but, I think, crucial moment within the life.

Another issue, this one a central concern, remains that of identifying the beginnings of a distinct Chicano autobiographic discourse. I might, for example, legitimately begin to trace the autobiographic tradition with the Spanish exploration narratives. I could argue that Columbus' *Journal* and *Carta* on the discovery of America are the first autobiographic accounts of life in the New World. Or that Hernán Cortez's *Cartas de relación* (1519–1526), Alvar Nuñez Cabeza de Vaca's *La Relación* (1542), Juan de Oñate's *Carta* and various *Relaciones* (1600–1628), Padre Eusebio Kino's *Relación sobre las misiones* (1710), and the scores of Franciscan missionary and settlement "Relaciones" of the 17th and 18th centuries all constitute the first autobiographies in the Americas that the Chicano, and other Americans, can claim as their own. After all, mainstream American literary historians have identified British travel narratives, histories, and theological discourse as the first literary productions of the nation; likewise, autobiography scholars have identified William Bradford's *Of Plymouth Plantation*, John Winthrop's *Journal* (1630–1649), Mary Rowlandson's *Narrative of Captivity* (1682), and numerous other histories and personal narratives as part of the nation's autobiographic tradition.[3] Both Spanish and British narratives constitute the beginnings of American literature since they express a literary response to the New World and were shaped by the experience in the Americas.[4]

On the other side of the Chicano's literary heritage scholars have already convincingly demonstrated that the indigenous literature of Mexico comprises another part of the Chicano literary tradition.[5] The literature that describes daily experience before the Spanish conquest, as well as much of that which records the Aztec response to the conquest, is often personalized and self-referring. This literature may perhaps be more analogically attuned to the Chicano's historical consciousness than that of the Spanish colonial period because it proceeds from the rupture experienced by Nahuatl society after the violence of the conquest. Even though many of these narratives are general accounts of the Spanish conquest, the autobiographicality of much in the Aztec *Codices* and the Mayan *Chilam Balam of Chumayel* is indisputable.[6]

While these texts function as part of the Chicano's literary heritage and can be read as autobiographical, I choose not to discuss them here because it seems to me that they are not in need of restoration, having been printed, many times in some cases, and read widely by scholars and general audiences. These texts have been disregarded by American scholars when establishing the literary canon for the nation and therefore still need to be argued into the literary tradition of this country. Moreover, they are usually read as historical documents rather than as autobiography and thus require analysis by scholars interested in the relationship between autobiography and historiographic texts. Nevertheless, the project may, I believe, be deferred without endangering an examination of the autobiography that succeeded the American occupation of northern Mexico in 1848. For it is the literature that was written after the Mexican American War of 1846–48 that has been silenced and which therefore comprises the literary missing link upon which consideration of recent literary activity must be based.

II

My point of intersection, then, for Chicano autobiographical literature is that historical moment when the United States violently appropriated northern Mexico in the mid-nineteenth century.[7] It was this event that set off social, political, economic, linguistic and cultural shockwaves which may be said to have generated an autobiographic impulse in Hispano-Mexicano society that constitutes a genuine autobiographical consciousness. I mean to say that the violent transformation of a well established society as much as forced many individuals into an autobiographic mode. Social rupture led to a decontextualization of individual and communal life that required a form of verbal restoration of that community with which the individual had identified his or her very locus of meaning. Before relocating life in the new regime, the life of the past had somehow to be accorded purpose, dignity, integrity. Autobiographic social history served this re-integrative, psycho-social process.

The earliest post-conquest narratives record, in their different forms (*memorias*, *apuntes*, *historias*, *reminiscencias*), the effects of the American takeover on the *mexicano* community in general and on individual experience specifically. Although much of the extant material upon which I base my study was composed by members of the upper, landowning classes, there are narratives that disclose the lives of common people—soldiers, working women, small ranchers, journalists. Regardless of class, however, these life histories are consciously coalescent articulations of individual and communal disjuncture. Whether embittered, confounded, acquiescent, resistant, self-denying, assertively defiant, they display a range of responses that mediate the nascent cultural and existential duality imposed upon *mexicanos* by a regime that mouthed a rhetoric of democratic ideals, but practiced unrelenting hostility in its relations with them. In fact, the contradiction between American democratic rhetoric and actual practice is often precisely the conflict that generates an autobiographic impulse which seeks to set the life into a context that will, through language and memory, illuminate and assign meaning to historical fracture and reconcile the individual to the reality of that fracture.

Beginning at mid-nineteenth century, a list of some of the autobiographical narratives composed out of this need to reconcile the self to a radically discontinuous history would include autobiographical material, most unpublished, some published but out of print for a century or more, collected from archives in Texas, New Mexico, and California, states that represent the largest population centers during the nineteenth century, as well as the three most distinct regions that met the onslaught of the occupation. Some of these autobiographical documents are the following: José Antonio Menchaca's "Reminiscencias" (1807–1836) and Juan Nepomuceno Seguíns' "Personal Memoirs" (1858) are highly ambivalent and often bitter defenses of their complicity in the Anglo Texas rebellion of 1836; Padre Antonio José Martínez, who was excommunicated by Archbishop Jean Baptiste-Lamy in 1861 (see Willa Cather's *Death Comes for the Archbishop*), composed an autobiographical narrative ("Relación") as early as 1836 and, during his feud with Lamy, wrote a number of self-referring tracts that may be considered autobiographical documents defending his clerical, political and personal behavior; Santiago Tafolla's "Nearing the End of the Trail" (ca. 1908) is the life history of a *mexicano* who spent his youth travelling in the eastern United States with an Anglo benefactor and then fought on the side of the South during the Civil War only to be forced to desert when he and fellow *mexicano* Confederate troops learned they were about to be lynched by white soldiers because they were "greasers"; the "Memoirs of Jesse Pérez" (1934), a Texas *mexicano* who, surprisingly enough, was a member of the Texas Rangers in the 1890's; José Policarpio Rodríguez's narrative "The Old Guide" (ca. 1897), like Tafolla's, describes his life as a trail guide and roustabout, and ends as a conversion narrative much in the Augustinian tradition; Raphael Chacón's "Memorias" (ca. 1912) is an account of his years as a member of the Union Army in New Mexico during the Civil War that may be read opposite Santiago Tafolla's; the exiled Mexican journalist Catarino Garza's "La lógica de los hechos" (1877–88), a provocative account of the ill-treatment of *mexicanos* in San Antonio in the last decades of the 19th Century.[8]

In California the largest single collection of 19th century personal narratives are those collected during the 1870's by the San Francisco bookdealer, document collector and professional historian, Hubert H. Bancroft, for his massive California history project. In this collection alone there are over one hundred *memorias, recuerdos históricos, reminiscencias, vidas,* etc. Most are oral histories collected by Bancroft's field researchers, the principals of whom were Enrique Cerruti and Thomas Savage, who, during a six year period from 1837–79, travelled a wide circuit from San Francisco to San Diego transcribing the lives of the "Californios," as the

"Californios," as the native California *mexicanos* were known. Among this collection, however, are a group of narratives, solicited by Bancroft, but composed alone or in guarded collaboration by individuals who wished to relate their personal and communal history in a manner that would secure them textual authority. Mariano Vallejo, Juan Bautista Alvarado, Antonio María Osío, Pío Pico were some of the men of wealth and considerable power in pre-American California who composed sustained historiographic narratives in which the "self" figures prominently into their description of social transformations that were displacing them even as they wrote. Mariano Vallejo's "Recuerdos históricos y personales tocante a la alta California" (1875),[9] for example, constitutes nearly one thousand pages of personal impressions of California society before and after the American occupation.

The Bancroft collection also contains a number of invaluable women's narratives that describe events during the Americanization of the territory from a distinctly feminine perspective. These narratives by women like María Angustias de la Guerra, Eulalia Pérez (a woman said to be 139 years old when her life story was recorded), Catarina Avila de Ríos, Apolinaria Lorenzana, offer significantly revealing views on gender relations in California society that variously criticize the patriarchal system that contained women's independence.

The narratives bequeathed by these individuals may have been used, and often misused, by Bancroft as social history, but it is the ever present "I" that transforms them from history proper into that genre of the life history—autobiography. Memory recovers history, and in recovering reshapes it, revises it, reassigns meaning to it, reinvents and repossesses it for the individual. The disclosure of individual experience and the overlay of individual personality upon the description of external socio-political realities, as well as the individuating of external events, mark these narratives with the distinct autobiographic authority.

III

Given what I have said about the narrative strategies deployed by *mexicano* autobiographers to revise damaging images of the cultural self, it is also necessary for Chicanos to assess and reconcile for ourselves the autobiographical evidence of cultural ambivalence, or more precisely, the cultural masking, that characterizes much Chicano autobiographical narrative. Since a good deal of the autobiography composed by *mexicanos* has been a sorting out of cultural identity, or identities, as well as a consideration of the position that individuals occupy, or are allowed to occupy, in American society, it should be no surprise to discover autobiographical texts inhabited by *mexicanos* posing as loyal Americans, who publicly shun their native culture, who denigrate other *mexicanos* for maintaining their language and cultural behaviors, who, in short, are embarrassingly self-denying. Such *mexicanos* have, from the moment a part of their nation collapsed in 1848, presented the spectacle of the cultural "other" trying various means of transformation into "Americans." Richard Rodriguez, author of the recently published and widely argued *Hunger of Memory* (1981),[10] is by no means the first Chicano autobiographer who has publicly disaffiliated himself from his culture in order to assume the mask of the "middle class" American. Rodriguez's autobiography has provoked a spate of commentary over the issue of cultural loyalty and the cultural individual's public, in this case, textual, responsibility to the group.[11] Such textual self-denial represents the desire to create a new self through language, as though to write oneself into a different life, to shed one skin for another through an incantation of self-describing words. The only obstacle to complete assimilation for such erstwhile "Americans" has been the hostile resistance on the part of those "real Americans" who, for instance, 150 years ago reminded Juan Nepomuceno Seguín that he could pen himself as "John" and drop his strange middle-name to "N," but that he was still just a "Mexican." Notwithstanding the incessant reminders of marginal social acceptance, however, a succession of *mexicanos* from Seguín to Richard Rodriguez have invented American personas with which they have sought to make their way in North American society.

Whether Rodriguez and his antecedents—a *mexicano* Confederate soldier, a *mexicano* Texas Ranger, or a culturally self-denying "Spanish-American" territorial governor—should be disavowed is an issue different readers must decide for themselves. However, precisely because their lives refuse to conform to some of the images we have created for ourselves, especially in recent years when we have radicalized that self image, their autobiographies do force us to recognize variations of the Chicano self. Reading Chicano autobiography from the last quarter of the nineteenth century forced me, at least, to expand the image of the *mexicano* I had constructed, an image which was obviously too easily divided between self-serving elites and humble working class *mexicanos*. I expected culturally ambivalent "Spanish-American" politicians—Seguín and Vallejo had prepared me for that. So, Miguel Antonio Otero, appointed Territorial Governor of New Mexico by President William McKinley in 1897,[12] came as no surprise. But a *mexicano* Confederate soldier? Never. That a *mexicano* would ever be part of the Confederacy had simply never crossed my mind; as it turns out there were many Confederate sympathizers in the *mexicano* community, especially in Texas, and, as I have discovered, at least two men—Santiago Tafolla and José Policarpio Rodríguez—who wrote about their experiences in the Gray. Even more surprising, no, dumbfounding, was the discovery of a *mexicano* Texas Ranger. I had simply assumed that the only relation between Texas Rangers and *mexicanos* was that of the lynch mob to its victims. Jesse Pérez's "Memoirs," however, provided a shock: Pérez was a member of one of the most anti-*mexicano* fascist groups in the Southwest, mostly for the money of course, but also because he liked thinking of himself as a Ranger. It allowed him to share in a power network from which *mexicanos* had been excluded, and, unfortunately, it constructed an ideological consciousness in him that largely alienated him from his own community.

I do not have time in this essay to discuss in any detail the autobiographies of either of these men. My purpose in introducing them, however, is to suggest the amount of work that is yet to be undertaken in the recovery and examination of Chicano autobiography. The continuation of the critical project in Chicano autobiography can be understood in light of the fact that José Policarpio Rodríguez's and Jesse Pérez's autobiographies raise distinct socio-ideological issues. Rodríguez's *"The Old Guide": His Life in His Own Words*, for instance, intends to be more than an account of his long experience as a soldier, scout, Indian fighter, ranchman and guide; it is, in the end, a traditional Protestant narrative of a sinner's life before his conversion. The central event of his life, as he records it, is his conversion, experienced in true Pauline fashion while he is riding his horse, and his subsequent decision to give up everything to preach the word of Christ. Therefore, in addition to its socio-political dimensions, clearly present throughout the text, the narrative must be examined for the configuration of spiritual life it seeks to identify.

In Pérez's case, his association and ideologic identification with the Rangers seem to indicate that perhaps he was "agringado" (assimilated) enough to have crossed the line, so to speak. Yet the language of his memoirs is, it seems to me, one of the most striking representations of thickly accented *mexicano* English I have ever read. No matter that he was a Ranger, he surely betrayed himself as a *mexicano* every time he opened his mouth. Would it be too speculative to think that Pérez was the unknowing dupe, the Mexican go-between who was used by the Rangers to effect their policies against *mexicanos* on either side of the border? I think not. Here, then, Pérez's autobiographic language complicates, actually subverts, autobiography intent. Moreover, whereas many other Rangers had their memoirs published,[13] Pérez was silenced, one suspects, because he sounded too much like a "Mexican." Such an image—a Mexican Texas Ranger —would simply not do, since it did not accord with the mythic figure of the Ranger as a tall, broad-shouldered, fair-skinned son of Texas who kept greasers, niggers, and other lawless vermin in their place.

In answer to the typical question offered by many—"But are there autobiographies written by Chicanos?"—I can now say that autobiography has recorded in manifold form and multi-voiced complexity the difficulty and diversity of our experience in North America. Although the archeological project itself is just beginning, it is an interpretive activity that will describe both the inter-cultural and intra-cultural forces that have shaped personal narrative. My celebratory mention of Chicano autobiography in such terms as "manifold form" and "multi-voiced complexity" is not meant to defray the issue of a contradictory ethos apparent in much autobiography. On the contrary, we must train ourselves upon such contradictions in order to arrive at a literary and cultural analysis that will make clearer the formation of our inherited literary discourse. Whether it be 19th century manuscripts long forgotten or more recently published but equally ignored life histories, the consideration of Chicano autobiography as a complex socio-ideologic narrative activity is a project that can no longer be delayed.

[1]Although there have more recently been a number of conference papers devoted to discussion of Chicano autobiographies, there are, to my knowledge, only three published essays, and all deal with autobiographies written within the last twenty years. See Genaro M. Padilla, "Self as Cultural Metaphor in Acosta's *The Autobiography of a Brown Buffalo,*" *Journal of General Education* 35, 4 (1984): 242-258; Antonio C. Marquez, "Richard Rodriguez's *Hunger of Memory* and the Poetics of Experience," *Arizona Quarterly*, Winter (1984): 130-141, and Ramón Saldívar, "Ideologies of Self: Chicano Autobiography," *Diacritics*, (Fall 1985): 25-34.

[2]There is, of course, a rather large body of critical literature that has moved well beyond a rigid definition of autobiography as a singularly self-disclosing text that reads something like St. Augustine's or Rousseau's *Confessions*. To follow Francis R. Hart, autobiography proper is no longer restricted to the construction of "a personal history that seeks to communicate or express the essential nature, the truth, of the self" ("Notes for an Anatomy of Modern Autobiography," *New Literary History*, 1 [1967-70]: 485-511, p. 491). Philippe Lejeune, on the contrary, defines autobiography as "a retrospective prose narrative produced by a real

person concerning his own existence, focusing on his individual life, in particular on the development of his personality" ("The Autobiographical Contract", *French Literary Theory Today*, Tzvetan Todorov, ed., (New York: Cambridge, 1982). Lejeune additionally insists that such forms as the memoir, diary and autobiographical poem do not properly satisfy the "conditions" of autobiography.

[3] See Daniel B. Shea, Jr., *Spiritual Autobiography in America* (Princeton, 1968); G. Thomas Couser, *American Autobiography: The Prophetic Mode* (Amherst: University of Massachusetts Press, 1979).

[4] As Philip D. Ortego eloquently argues in "Background of Mexican American Literature" (Ph.D. dissertation, University of New Mexico, 1971), "In the pluralistic cultural and linguistic con text of contemporary America we can no longer consent to accept unquestioningly the kinds of pat openings used by American literary historians suggesting that American literature begins properly with the arrival of British colonials in America. For the fact of the matter is that American literature actually begins with the formation of the United States as a political entity. Thus, the literary period from the founding of the first permanent British settlement at Jamestown, Virginia, in 1607, to the formation of the American Union, properly speaking, represents the British period of American literature. So, too, the literary period from the first Spanish settlement at Saint Augustine, Florida, in 1565, to the dates of acquisition of those Spanish and Mexican lands by the United States should in fact represent the Hispanic period in American literature. More appropriately, the British and Spanish periods could be tagged under the rubric of 'Colonial American Literature.' " (pp. 24-25.)

[5] See Philip D. Ortego's "Backgrounds" (cited above), pp. 25-29; Tomás Ybarra-Frausto, "Alurista's Poetics: The Oral, the Bilingual, The Pre-Columbian," *Modern Chicano Writers: A Collection of Critical Essays* (Englewood Cliffs, NJ: Prentice Hall, 1979), Joseph Sommers and Tomás Ybarra-Frausto; Egla Morales Blovin, "Símbolos y motivos nahuas en la literatura chicana," in *The Identification and Analysis of Chicano Literature* (New York: Bilingual Press, 1979), Francisco Jiménez, ed.; Jorge Huerta, *Chicano Theater: Themes and Forms* (Ypsilanti, Michigan: Bilingual Press, 1982).

[6] Miguel León-Portilla, *Las literaturas precolumbinas de México*, (Mexico: Editorial Pormaca, 1964), *The Broken Spears: Aztec Account of the Conquest of Mexico* (Boston: Beacon Press, 1961, 1966); José María Vigil, *Nezahualcoyotl, el rey poeta*, (Mexico: Ediciones de Andrea, 1957); *The Book of Chilam Balam of Chumayel*, (Norman, Oklahoma: University of Oklahoma Press, 1967).

[7] For useful accounts of the Mexican American War, as well as the social, political, cultural transformations that resulted see: Carey McWilliams' *North From Mexico: The Spanish-Speaking People of the United States* (New York: Greenwood Press, 1968), Rodolfo Acuña's *Occupied America: A History of Chicanos* (New York: Harper & Row, 1981), Leonard Pitt's *The Decline of the Californios: A Social History of the Spanish-Speaking Californians, 1846-1890* (Los Angeles: University of California Press, 1966).

[8] Menchaca's "Reminiscencias" (MS, typescript), Seguín's "Personal Mem-

oirs" (typescript), Pérez's "Memoirs" (typescript), Tafolla's "Nearing the End of the Trail" (MS), and Garza's "La lógica de los hechos" (MS), are housed in the University of Texas Library, Austin; Rodriguez, *"The Old Guide": His Life in His Own Words* (Dallas, Texas, Methodist Church, ca. 1897); Padre Martínez's "Relación de Méritos," first published by Martínez himself in 1836, may be found in the Benjamin Read Papers, State Records Center, Santa Fe, New Mexico, and also in translation in the *New Mexico Historical Review*, October 1928, Cecil Romero, trans.; Chacón's "Memorias" (MS) is housed in the Norling Library, Historical Collections, University of Colorado, Boulder.

[9]Volume 1-5, Manuscript Collection, Bancroft Library; see also Earl R. Hewitt, typescript translation, "Historical and Personal Memoirs Relating to Alta California," Manuscript Collection, Bancroft Library.

[10]*Hunger of Memory: The Education of Richard Rodriguez* (Boston: David R. Godie, 1981).

[11]*Hunger of Memory* has received hostile reviews from most Chicano critics while it has, in general, been favorably reviewed by Anglos. The manner in which Rodriguez's book has been received by two different interpretive communities is the subject of an essay I am in the process of completing. See, for example, Cordelia Candelaria's *"Hang-Up of Memory: Another View of Growing Up Chicano,"* *The American Book Review* 5:4, (May-June, 1983): 4; Paul Zweig, "The Child of Two Cultures," *The New York Times Book Review*, April 5, 1982, p.1.

[12]Although not published until this century, Miguel Antonio Otero's autobiographical trilogy *My Life on the Frontier, 1864-1882*, Vol. 1 (New York: Press of the Pioneers, 1935), *My Life on the Frontier, 1882-1897* (Albuquerque: University of New Mexico, 1939), and *My Nine Years as Governor of the Territory of New Mexico, 1897-1905* (Albuquerque: University of New Mexico, 1940) is a lengthy account of Otero's rise to national prominence during the late territorial period in New Mexico.

[13]A short list of gringo Texas Ranger memoirs published around the time Pérez composed his 144 page memoir include the following: James B. Gillet's *Six Years with the Texas Rangers, 1875-81* (New Haven: Yale, 1925); Claude L. Douglas' *The Gentlemen in the White Hats: Dramatic Episodes in the History of the Texas Rangers* (Dallas, Texas: Southwest Press, 1934); Jennings Napoleon Augustus' *A Texas Ranger* (Dallas, Texas: Turner College, 1930).

Mediators and Mediation in Rudolfo Anaya's Trilogy:
Bless Me, Ultima, Heart of Aztlán and Tortuga.

Jean Cazemajou
University of Bordeaux

As Roland Barthes insistently pointed out in his theoretical writings, "l'écriture" is a grid of "sociolects," that is to say "group discourse" or competing languages which are finally drawn by the author, more or less skillfully, into a complex signifying web. This is why the French critic rejected the notion of style as the servant of content: everything, as he saw it, was indivisibly present in "l'écriture." "Form" and "content" were mere gadgets used by old-fashioned critics and, in Barthes' own approach to the text, had to be considered as inseparable.[1]

We shall consider Anaya's trilogy, whose publication covers a period of seven years, as a good demonstration of the validity of Barthes' conception of literature. This sequence of texts reveals an interesting evolution, through the seventies, in which Anaya has successfully responded to the various cultural and aesthetic forces at work in him, shaping and reshaping his system of communication with the reader. One constant, however, has remained striking in his prose: the author of the trilogy, unlike many modern writers, is not trying to erect artificial barriers between reader and story-teller; he wished, on the contrary, to be the perfect mediator. His trilogy forms a closely interwoven network of narratives set in a *real* locale, northern New Mexico, but also in a mythical universe organized around primordial archetypes: the river, the mountain, the sea, the windswept plain, the goat-path, the bridge, the sun, the moon, to name only the most frequently recurrent. His characters are all products of these specific settings, especially in *Bless Me, Ultima*, where the main source of the young protagonist's dilemma is a conflict between two cultural heritages, that of the Lunas —a race of farmers and peace-loving people— and that of the Márezes—a race of conquistadors brought by the sea— whose respective bloods mingled giving birth to him.

The religion with which these stories are inbued encounters Catholic ritual on its way but has in part outgrown this heritage and persistently seeks a mystic relationship with the earth. A "sense of place," a total harmony with the "raw, majestic and awe inspiring landscape of the southwest"² is the prime mover of the creative process. The vanguard point from which Anaya observes life is "the land of the eagle and the nopal" and, beyond the *llano*, the blue mountains (*Heart of Aztlán*, p. 8). His major characters are not one-dimensional and their psychological definition extends far beyond the boundaries of his native New Mexico. Among them, however, are local color types, the *vaquero*, the farmer, often uprooted and ill-at-ease in an urban setting, the moderately successful Chicano businessman, the priest, the youth in search of God and his own identity, the conservative father, the loving mother, the village or barrio outcast, the *vato loco*, the *pachuco*, the liberated adolescent girl, the exploited worker and the community leader. Towering over them looms the figure of the mediator, Ultima in *Bless Me, Ultima*, Crispín in *Heart of Aztlán*, and Ismelda in *Tortuga*, who preserve an indispensable contact with the world of Nature and the supernatural forces inhabiting this universe which, as the Indians say, have always been with us. The mediator plays a role similar to that of the *santero* in contemporary forms of Caribbean religious practice. He or she is not a natural leader but merely there to inspire or guide potential leaders or future mediators. Community life would not be what it is without the presence of the various mediators, the major ones, already mentioned, and their apprentices and assistants like Salomón in *Tortuga* who relay the magic power dormant in Nature and transmute it into beneficent action. The group in which they operate is fairly homogeneous: it is a society of *mestizos* and Indians, and the Anglos, even if they are close by, tend to live by themselves.

Mediation for a writer is linked with the problem of the instrumentality and scope of literary communication. Anaya's first target is an audience of *compadres*, who seem to need little explanation, but he has also in mind a larger audience waiting somewhere to hear the author's voice. As a Chicano novelist he is fully conscious that he is addressing both at the same time. In an interview that he gave in 1979 he pointed out this universal goal of his: "[. . .] In taking responsibility for my own actions and my own creation, I therefore take responsibility for everyone in all of the universe."³

The first instrument that he uses is the power of ancient myths, so well dramatized in many legends and *cuentos* of New Mexico but already present in those primordial images that Jung called "the Great Mother" and "the archetypal light."⁴

This power is conveyed to the reader by means of Anaya's best literary tool—a language which is both direct and spontaneous but which has also been very minutely and carefully crafted to give his stories a very specific *flavor*. Code-switching from English to Spanish and vice-versa is used more and more sparingly as the trilogy develops, and Spanish seems to be almost entirely absent from the narrative sequences and the dialogues in *Tortuga*, but it keeps operating at a submerged level with the use of many characters' names, occasional references to local realities which are given Spanish names or have a Spanish identity and, above all, by the persistent use of Aztec and Pueblo mythologies. Events marked by a great emotional charge such as Tortuga's acquisition of a wheelchair, a major stage in his gradual recovery, are usually greeted by a burst of song or an upsurge of exclamations *in Spanish*. In this case Tortuga's best friends belt out the famous Mexican revolutionary song "La Cucaracha." In the two previous novels, which are closer to everyday life in the village or the barrio, the presence of Spanish is more visible and serves to convey a certain community spirit through systematic use of *oral* language, with such identity markers as "órale," "ése," "Hijo de la chingada!" What Anaya captures best is not just the diglottic situation but the flavor of a certain culture, the way in which daily life in New Mexico is constantly "*traversed*"—to use one of Barthes's favorite terms—by the effects of a pervasive mythological imagination. Characters tend to live in two separate worlds at the same time: in the visible world of tangible reality, often brutal and always linked with the cycle of the seasons, and in a world of dreams, premonitions and *folklore* in the authentic sense of popular lore. Crispín, for example, in *Heart of Aztlán*, is a blind barrio musician, provided with an extraordinary skill in playing the guitar and in using this instrument to express all the emotions triggered by the major events of life: birth, maturity, conflict and death. But he is also an archetypal figure—a sort of Homeric bard whose best treasures are invisible and seem to stem from an undefined divine source which has, in any case, close links with the earth and the world of Nature. In the same novel Clemente is first an ordinary farmer, uprooted and lost in the labyrinth of urban mores but, thanks to Crispín's aid, he too will be "traversed" by myth and raised to the status of mediator. As beneficiary and agent of the mediation process, he then participates at the same time of the plumed serpent's duality—heaven and earth combined—but also of the same duality in Christian mythology: "Christ the man being also Christ the God."[5]

The second level at which mediation operates is that of the *texture* of the writer's creation, the mysterious concatenation of stylistic effects which can never fully catch up with the game the author is after—a game that critics have called "significance" or "message." Epiphany in language, as Roland Barthes very perceptively pointed out, is always a mirage, but, on some rare occasions, the author reaches those peaks of wisdom on which can be heard what Barthes calls "the rustle of language"[6]—a phonic equivalent of the "small pregnant suns" that seem to float in the spread tail of the peacock that Flannery O'Connor used as a loaded symbol in "The Displaced Person." It is in *Tortuga* that Anaya best uses the resources of his language as a writer, and the felicity of this literary artifact is, at times, reminiscent of Barthes's utopian dream of the "rustle of language" in epiphany.

The third and more dramatic level of mediation is psychological: it gives Anaya's fiction shamanic overtones and brings into play the various mediators, acting as shamans and their assistants within the framework of individual stories. All of them are ordinary people with a touch of the divine in them and, through magic or healing gifts, attempt to pull their disciples and *protégés* out of the devil's hands where evil forces have inexorably thrown them. The dichotomy of Anaya's moral universe may strike the sophisticated reader as simplistic, but he is not the only contemporary writer to have warned us, moderns, about this return of Satan in a world that we thought liberated once and for all of such superstitions.

In order to address the problem raised by the first level of mediation, which is that of myth, i.e., that of deeply felt communal beliefs in a community whose awareness of myth has to be revived, it will be necessary to turn to what the writer himself and other Chicano authors have said on this question. Anaya's mythopoesis uses myths linked to a pre-Columbian cosmogony. Besides the divine powers associated with the sun and the moon in this world vision, he constantly returns to the Nahuatl veneration of the quincunx with its symbolic representation of an ideal center. When he said, at a "round table" of Chicano writers in 1981, "I define myth as the truth in the heart'"[7]—a definition challenged by Alejandro Morales on strictly classical Jungian terms—he was trying to universalize the concept of myth, but he also pointed out, on this occasion, the specific contribution made by Chicano literature to a rediscovery of unifying archaic values that mainstream American literature had failed to provide. María Herrera-Sobek, Alurista and Alejandro Morales then presented their own conceptions of the role of myth in literature and contemporary life. Alurista remarked that some of the myths Chicanos had tried to use—those of Christianity, for instance—had not proved very useful. He supported, however, the myth of Aztlán which functioned, according to him, as a "unifying tool" in the present Chicano struggle, but added that it should not "become an opiate." Morales emphasized the positive value of myth in the creation of an authentic Chicano literary production and Herrera-Sobek reminded the audience that Chicanos had "followed a pattern that Mexico had established" during their revolution, i.e. "revived [their] past."⁸ The final point made by Anaya was that myth was perhaps neglected or derided by postmodernism but it might very well function as the survival kit of our world—a conflictual universe, plagued by fragmentation and fascinated by the prospect of self-destruction.

Anaya's great familiarity with mesoamerican mythologies and his early immersion in mainstream American literature place his work at the meeting point of numerous literary traditions. In the trilogy he elaborated a complex network of events which may find their origin in ancient legends but which are always adapted to modern circumstances. Writing as he does in a period which has seen the central values of his Mexican heritage rediscovered with considerable pride, he is inevitably drawn to the myth of Aztlán, launched by Alurista in 1969 and which acquired official status in the Movement with the Denver Conference of 1969.⁹

Associated with the bitter reality of dispossession and oppression by a hostile Anglo culture, it operates as a magic spring-board for Anaya's imagination: the merging of the eagle and the serpent in Aztec mythology was revived by him in *Heart of Aztlán* where two mythic animals exchange roles with the steel snakes of the exploitative railroad and the eagle-eyed leader of the strike (*Heart of Aztlán*, pp. 84, 86). And the search for Aztlán, seen as a sort of lost paradise, becomes in this novel, a pilgrimage to the magic mountain teaching the potential leader that the real Aztlán is not a geographical place but a feeling of spiritual union with his people, buried deep in his heart.

Anaya wrote in 1977, "My interest in writing is to explore the magic in realism."¹⁰ One year later, interviewed by Juan Bruce-Novoa, he defined his position with a mixture of firmness and moderation:

> "The role of a writer is vis-a-vis the universe itself. Chaos versus pattern. I fit easily and completely into the Chicano community—that's where I was born and raised, that's where my family resides—and the Movement, because I was active in it and have seen its different areas of development. I think that in part I fit into the mainstream society, what you call U.S. society."¹¹

Besides its mythic structure, Anaya's language is characterized by its highly individualized *texture* which strikes the observant reader by the recurrence of occasional outburst: of the vernacular enwrapped in a melodic flow where sophistication prevails. *Heart of Aztlán*, for instance, reads like a musical composition and the haunting figure of Crispín, "the man with the blue guitar," remains branded in our memory once the book is closed. He blends together into a felicitous harmony a great many strands of thought and emotion and exerts a powerful influence not only on the barrio but also on the reader. His blue guitar is the depository of ancient mysteries and legends, and this legacy of a remote Indian past finds its best expression in the passages printed in italics which form a mythic counterpoint to the narrative. This novel is a kind of symphony which incorporates elements from many sources outside Aztec and Pueblo mythologies. One may be surprised to find that it owes a literary debt to Wallace Stevens—to some critics, the very embodiment of aesthetic hedonism, but an artist highly respected by Anaya as "one of the major poets of the imagination."[12] In a more subdued manner, another voice seems to me audible in this novel, that of Stephen Crane: the presence in this writer's work of a passion for the open spaces of the West can also be found in Anaya's fiction, both authors tending to perceive landscape in archetypal terms.

Anaya's interest in Wallace Stevens, as reflected in *Heart of Aztlán*, is linked to two poems, "The Man with the Blue Guitar" (1973) and "The Comedian as the Letter C" (1923)—a poem whose central character is a voyager called Crispín. This character does not resemble Anaya's Crispín physically or psychologically, but both Crispins are confronted with the same problem—that of man's relation with the world of external reality. The opening lines of Stevens' poem:

> "Nota: man is the intelligence of his soil,
> The sovereign ghost. . . . " (*O.P.*, p. 30)

In typical Wallace Stevens fashion this lead to a counter statement approximating what Anaya calls his "sense of place."

> "Nota: his soil is man's intelligence.
> That's better. That's worth crossing seas to find." (*O.P.* p. 30).

Both Stevens and Anaya tend to emphasize the physicality of an authentic knowledge of the world, but there is, in the latter, a more sincere need for what he calls "epiphany in landscape,"[13] that is to say something very close to religious experience. In *Heart of Aztlán*, Crispín borrows his shamanic features from Wallace Stevens' "The Man with the Blue Guitar" and his name from "The Comedian as the Letter C." In Anaya's story Crispín's guitar, "carved from the heart of a juniper tree," has come to replace "the flutes of the priests" and thus become a cultural symbol of the Chicano community: "It was a new instrument, a subterfuge, passing from poet it wove that future out of things as they are" (*Heart of Aztlán*, p. 27). We can hear there a distant but distinct echo of Stevens' poem, "The Man with the Blue Guitar" in which the anonymous speaker says,

"Poetry
Exeeding music must take the place
Of empty heaven and its hymns,

Ourselves in poetry must take their place
Even in the chattering of your guitar." (*S.P.*, p. 54)

And the phrase "things as they are" runs like a burden throughout Stevens' poem, dialectically contrasted with the artist's creative imagination. In Anaya's novel, Crispín is not merely an anonymous barrio musician but an archetypal blind man provided with clairvoyance and supernatural healing powers, both mediator and shaman, whereas Father Cayo, Barelas' acting priest, is inefficient and hypocritical. Crispín indeed officiates at all major ceremonies in the barrio. Exposure to the sun blinded him when he crossed the desert to move from Mexico to "the land the ancients called Aztlán" (*Heart of Aztlán*, p. 28), i.e., from the present to the past, in this pilgrimage, to the sources of his being. But ironically he knows and sees everything. He is the one around whom the community gathers to celebrate the arrival of the Chávez family in the city. His guitar has the same power as that of his counterpart in Wallace Stevens' poem who says:

"And things are as I think they are
And say they are on the blue guitar." (*S.P.*, p. 70)

This statement is echoed by Crispín's remark in Chapter 1 of *Heart of Aztlán*: "Things as they are never appear the same on the blue guitar." (*Heart of Aztlán*, p. 14)

In Anaya's trilogy this instrument is a talisman handed down from one barrio bard to the next. Jason's younger brother, Benjie, learns, in *Tortuga*, through a letter from his mother that Crispín has just died but left him his guitar, and Salomón, his mentor in the hospital, tells him that it is now *"his turn"* to sing and play this magic instrument for his people (*Tortuga*, p. 171). Thus the line of shamanic priests can go uninterrupted. During the fall following the Chávez family move to Barelas a wildcat strike erupts in the barrio. Crispín plays his guitar again and initiates the workers to the legend of Aztlán: the war god of the Aztecs had once prepared them for the choice of a permanent settlement in their exodus from the north, telling them to watch for a sign—an eagle eating a serpent while perched on a cactus. This symbolic image—now the emblem of the Mexican Republic—is, in *Heart of Aztlán*, adapted to a modern context, the serpent representing the odious power of the railroad company and the eagle the "savior" sent by the guardian sun, Clemente Chávez. At his stage in his psychological development Clemente is only dimly aware of what is expected of him, but Crispín will show him the way. After climbing the magic mountain, Clemente will do more than just relate to this mysterious country called Aztlán, the former home of his ancestors. He will suddenly realize that "HE [IS] AZTLAN," in other words, that harmony between him and his universe is perfect (*Heart of Aztlán*, p. 131). With the help of Crispín he will find his way back to the barrio and carry out his predestined task.

In the concluding episode of the book Crispín appears again. After the fall of Benjie, Jason's brother, from a water tank that Sapo, a pachuco from another gang, had forced him to climb, Crispín plays on his guitar "the music of life" (Ibid., p. 202) and Benjie escapes death but seems condemned to remain paralyzed. Then in the very last section of the story, Clemente, outstaging Lalo, the radical, leads his people to the accompaniment of Crispín's guitar playing a "tune of liberation" (Ibid., p. 208). The goal pursued by the strikers and their mystic leader remains rather vague but, poetically, the passage is beautiful. The strikers move forward like a river "cutting its new channel into the future" (Ibid.). Music is the unifying element of the narrative and Crispín's guitar truly functions as a rallying point and a source of inspiration.

The interplay between Stephen Crane's work and *Heart of Aztlán* is more tenuous but worth exploring just the same. To hint at any kind of relationship between Anaya and Crane may seem rather odd but Anaya himself said in an interview that "in the beginning he had the U.S. American novels to work with, "not the Mexican models.[14]
He thus encountered Crane's work at a very early age. Like Crane, Anaya is extremely sensitive to his physical environment and both writers are inclined to use the "forces in [their] landscape"[15]
for aesthetic and symbolic purposes. To Crane the impressionist, landscape had a lot to do with the effects of sunlight on the greens, browns and grays of Nature at all times of day. But, to Crane the Jungian writer, the sun was an archetype associated with fire and blood—something that Anaya has probably internalized through his immersion in Aztec mythology. The famous line concluding chapter nine of *The Red Badge of Courage*, after Jim Conklin's horrible "danse macabre," "The red sun was pasted in the sky like a wafer" (W., Vol. I, p. 98) which, in the first draft, read "like a fierce wafer," and Crane's reference to war as "the red animal, the blood-swollen god" (W., pp. 51-52) call to mind the human sacrifices required in the Nahuatl religion to placate the Aztec's fierce battle god and sun diety, Huitzilopochtli. Anaya's striking simile in chap-

ter one of *Heart of Aztlán*, "The sun hung like a gold medallion in the blue sky" (*Heart of Aztlán*, p. 6), appearing as it does after the violent death of Guillermo, Clemente's brother, has a Cranean ring to it.

In another and later passage Anaya relates for us the ritual rumble between the pachucos and the stompers on the occasion of The State Fair. We can detect there, in the tone of the narrative, the same gentle irony that Crane leveled at his would-be hero, another youth tormented by the problem of manly conduct under stress. The narrator captures the right note of equivocal pride in the young pachucos when they return home after the battle.

> "They laughed and entered their barrio proudly, carrying their wounds like badges of courage." (*Heart of Aztlán*, p. 98)

Anaya often resorts to totemic animals that play important roles in the symbolic framework of his stories. It is the case in *Bless Me, Ultima*, where the owl—a bird associated with the god of the netherworld in Aztec mythology and with Ultima in the novel—operates as an interesting fusion of contraries, both tutelary spirit and messenger of death. In *Tortuga* the same union of opposites is found in the turtle, earth-ridden and, at the same time, associated with the magic mountain bearing its name, hence with heavenward aspirations. The golden deer racing across the sky in *Heart of Aztlán* combines the positive qualities of the most useful animal in Pueblo culture and the centrality of the sun in Aztec mythology. Above all, it stands for the fifth sun—the sun of movement and cosmic unity.

This Indian heritage clashes with Spanish Catholicism which pervades the three stories. Tony's conventional Catholic education fails to satisfy his great sensitivity and his common sense, and an Indian faith, revived by Ultima, soon competes with the official religion.

The three novels are closely interrelated. Although Chávez' name is not mentioned in *Tortuga*, the protagonist is Jason's younger brother, Benjie, paralyzed by the accident he suffered in *Heart of Aztlán*. Encased in a heavy plaster cast, he is completing, in a hospital for crippled children, his shamanic training with the help of Imelda, a young nurse who relays to him the messages of the magic mountain. The physical aspect of the rebirth myth has its spiritual counterpart when Benjie leaves the hospital; he is cradling in his arms the blue guitar that Crispín sent him before he died: both body and soul have thus been liberated.

In *Bless Me, Ultima* several characters act as positive mediators and their teachings are dramatized by means of the ten Jungian dreams that serve to guide Tony in his initiatory journey. The young protagonist is at the intersection of the two vectors, receiving and giving at the same time:

he participates in Ultima's magic practices as an assistant but is entirely on his own when he gives a dying man the last rites. The shamanic journey in the three stories includes images of ascent and heavenward flight.[16] Ultima's last wish provides a good illustration of this patter: she orders Tony to "take the owl, go west into the hills" (*Bless Me, Ultima*, p. 247) and bury the totemic bird under a forked juniper tree. When he has carried out this task, he knows that Ultima's *soul* is safe. The other members of his family can then give her *body* a Catholic burial.

Some critics have found Anaya's depiction of what he calls "the indigenous people"[17] somewhat romantic and have objected to his refusal of "any narrow ideology"[18]. The second objection is irrelevant since myth, not militancy, is his major literary tool. As to the former, it is not justified either, since his "romantic" turn of mind enables him to eschew the pitfalls of naturalism that await most minority writers. Language, as a system of signs—sometimes akin to music—remains his first priority. He is inclined to reserve Spanish for references to family or community bonds, prayers and curses, and occasional forays into magic, but English predominates. Whereas Chicano poetry has remained the best instrument of political challenge and was even called by Rafael Jesús González "our Huitzilopochtli,"[19] some Chicano novelists have tried to come to terms with their mixed heritage and their paradoxical "exile" on their ancestors' land. This attempt at a synthesis has not always been successful, but Anaya's trilogy, with its advocacy of mutual love and comradeship as the best instruments of mediation, occupies a privileged niche in a literature which is warm, dynamic and spiritually alive.

[1]See, for example, his analysis of "Sarrasine"—a Balzac short story in *S/Z* (Paris: Editions du Seuil, 1970).

[2]Rudolfo Anaya, "A Writer Discusses His Craft", *CEA Critic* 40 (Nov. 1977), p. 40.

[3]David Johnson and David Apodaca, "Myth and the Writer: A Conversation with Rudolf Anaya", *New America* 3 (Spring 1979) p. 80.

[4]Carl Jung. *Four Archetypes* (Princeton, N.J.: Princeton University Press, Bollingen paperback, 1970), p. 9.

[5]*New America*, loc.cit., p. 81.

[6]"Le bruissement de la langue" in *Essais critiques IV, Le bruissement de la langue* (Paris: Ed. du Seuil, 1984), pp. 94–95.

[7]"Mitólogos y Mitómanos" (mesa redonda con Alurista, R. Anaya, M. Herrera-Sobek, A. Morales y H. Viramontes), *Maize* 4 (Spring-Summer 1981), p. 11.

[8] *Ibid.*, pp. 8, 11, 15.

[9] Luis Leal, "In Search of Aztlán", *Denver Quarterly* 16 (Fall 1981), pp. 16-22.

[10] *CEA Critic*, loc. cit., p. 40.

[11] Juan Bruce-Novoa, *Chicano Authors: Inquiry by Interview* (Austin, TX: University of Texas Press, 1981), p. 190.

[12] César González, "An Interview of Rudolfo Anaya" by César A. González, San Diego, CA, Sunday, March 31, 1985, ms., p. 4.

[13] Rudolfo Anaya, "The Writer's Landscape: Epiphany in Landscape", *Latin American Literary Review* 5 (Spring-Summer 1977), pp. 98-102.

[14] Bruce-Novoa, op.cit., p. 191.

[15] *CEA Critic*, loc.cit, p. 41.

[16] Mircea Eliade, *Mythes, reves et mystere* (Paris: Gallimard, 1957), pp. 126-154, in chp. 6 "Le vol magique".

[17] "Mitólogos y Mitómanos", loc.cit., p. 23.

[18] Bruce-Novoa, op.cit., p. 191.

[19] Rafael Jesús González, "Chicano Poetry/Smoking Mirror," in Ricardo Romo and Raymund Paredes, eds., *New Directions in Chicano Scholarship* (University of California at Santa Barbara: Center for Chicano Studies, 1984), p. 136.

N.B. The editions used for Anaya's trilogy are: *Bless Me, Ultima* (Berkeley, CA: Tonatiuh International, 1972); *Heart of Aztlán* (Berkeley, CA: Editorial Justa, 1976); *Tortuga* (Berkeley, CA: Editorial Justa, 1979). For Wallace Stevens, *Selected Poems* (London: Faber, 1953) for "The Man with the Blue Guitar" and *Opus Posthumous* (N.Y.: Knopf, 1957) ed. by S.F. Morses for "The Comedian as the Letter C." For Stephen Crane, *The Work of Stephen Crane*, ed. by Wilson Follett (N.Y.: Knopf, 1925-27, reissued by Russell & Russell, 1963).

The Establishment of Community in Zora Neale Hurston's *The Eatonville Anthology* (1926) and Rolando Hinojosa's *Estampas del valle* (1973)

Heiner Bus
University of Mainz

In his essay "Chicano Literature: The Establishment of Community,"[1] Tomás Rivera defined community as "place, values, personal relationships, and conversation"[2] and subsequently described two short pieces by Rolando Hinojosa as "attempts to build a community."[3] In the final paragraph he generalized this observation:

> Up to the present time, one of the most positive things that the Chicano writer and Chicano literature have conveyed to our people is the development of such a community. We have a community today (at least in literature) because of the urge that existed and because the writers actually created from a spiritual history, a community captured in words and in square objects we call books.

The urge to create a community, in and through literature, should be conceded not only to the Chicanos. To reveal correspondences and divergences in two ethnic literatures, I shall analyze two texts with obvious structural and thematic similarities, Zora Neale Hurston's "The Eatonville Anthology" published in 1926[5] and Rolando Hinojosa's "Estampas del valle", part of his first major work, *Estampas del valle y otras obras* (1973).[6] After the two analytical sections I will compare the two cycles[7] and determine their place in the context of Hurston's and Hinojosa's other works. In the end I very tentatively shall try to distinguish them from mainstream products treating the same theme.

In his *Zora Neale Hurston. A Literary Biography*[8] Robert E. Hemenway highly praises "The Eatonville Anthology":

> It is pure Zora Neale Hurston: part fiction, part folklore, part biography, all told with great economy, an eye for authentic detail, and a perfect ear for dialect . . . It is Hurston's most effective attempt at representing the original tale-telling context . . . the best written representation of her oral art.[9]

"The Eatonville Anthology" consists of fourteen individual pieces. In contrast to Edgar Lee Master's *Spoon River Anthology* (1915)[10] the titles of the sections[11] do not disclose an apparent ordering device,[12] although the combination of place name and "anthology" implies a deeper kinship between the two works, particularly their view of small-town life as a feature of the past.

Most of the fourteen sections open with a statement on the outstanding quality of a character which defines his social status.[13] Whenever this introduction refers to a negative quality, the narrator rushes to the character's help with a modification such as "Coon Taylor never did any stealing"[14] or an extensive explanation like:

> Becky Moore has eleven children of assorted colors and sizes. She has never been married, but that is not her fault. She has never stopped any of the fathers of her children from proposing, so if she has no father for her children it's not her fault. The men round about are entirely to blame.[15]

By this strategy the narrator signals approval of these individual attitudes and the responses of the community: stealing Coon Taylor has to "leave his town for three months"[16] only. In the case of Becky Moore the women of the town isolate her children to prevent contamination. Only the town vamp, Daisy Taylor, eventually leaves for good after overstepping the limits of the townspeople's tolerance. But even here the narrator closes in an ironic and conciliatory tone: "Before the week was up, Daisy moved to Orlando. There in a wider sphere, perhaps, her talents as a vamp were appreciated."[17]

Without deeply probing the psyche or the history of these figures,[18] the narrator and the citizens of Eatonville pragmatically consider even the self-imposed isolation of some of its members constituent for their community. This fact accounts for the static, anti-climactic nature of the place and its portrayal. In hardly any of the stories are the basic situations subject to change. We learn of some unsuccessful efforts in the past to correct obvious iniquities. Generally, however, people just feel amused and entertained like the prospective reader or listener.[19]

The World War, the coming of the railroad, and the departure of individuals occasionally cause physical and spiritual movement depicted as the loosening of morals and the questioning of social rituals. Only when these phenomena endanger institutions guaranteeing the survival of the community do people start reacting: The women e.g. violently defend the family. Normally, the communal self-defense mechanisms are still functioning. Change but complicates matters as the narrator indicates: "Back to the good old days before the World War, things were simple in

Eatonville."[20] Continuity is felt or at least pretended within a generation and between the older and younger ones.[21] The general refusal to examine the many dimensions of an individual character perfectly matches with this denial of change by eagerly overrating the stereotypical, the communal rituals. The reader perceives change mainly as a function of biological processes, i.e., the eventual death of the people portrayed.

Though the narrator makes frequent use of irony, he basically shares the attitudes and values of Eatonville. Quite often he adapts his syntax and vocabulary to the plainness of what he is telling. The repetition of words, phrases and situations, the narrator's and his figure's falling back on proverbial wisdom, expose the ritualistic quality of the experience. In the "Village Fiction" sequence the narrator even joins the lying contest with one of the town characters. Nevertheless, his command of various language registers signals detachment.[22] With the exception of the closing formula, Black English is exclusively used whenever the characters are allowed to speak up for themselves. With evident delight in verbalization and in the tasks of the arranger he draws Eatonville as a collection of types permanently re-enacting stereotypical social encounters, thus assigning to this community permanence and continuity, affirming his characters' desire to resist fundamental change.

The selection and positive acknowledgment of repetitive social action as a typical feature of a small Black community is based on a profound respect for individual conduct and a deep trust in the correspondence of human emotions. Hurston closes her "Anthology" with a Brer Rabbit tale explaining why the dog and rabbit hate each other.[23] In contrast to the preceding "crayon enlargements of life,"[24] the folk tale displays a firm cause-and-effect relationship. But it refers to a collective, not an individual phenomenon of the animal world, detached from a specific time and place. It is set "Once way back yonder before the stars fell."[25] Projecting human behavior into the animal world signifies a reality-thinking desire, an effort to conjure up imperial power in a situation of oppression.

These observations should make us see the stabilizing functions of storytelling as demonstrated in the folk tale and the whole "Anthology". By closing with a brer Rabbit story, Hurston transfers its strengths and weaknesses to her portrait of a specific community. The formula "Stepped on a tin, mah story ends" lifts the spell on the folk tale and the whole cycle whose individual themes and situations were already adapted to the typical features of the folk tale. The re-construction of Eatonville as a community establishes a complex interrelation between the narrator and his material and an equally strong communion between storyteller and his prospective audiences; it is folklore in the making. Storytelling is as repetitive as the situations re-enacted and described. Zora Neale Hurston hints at the importance of cultural identity through ritualization in "Double-Shuffle" where the males turn the formal dancing into a celebration of the Black musical folk traditions. Before releasing the listener into his own ambiguous world, the process of selection, verbalization and repetition, affirming and denying the restrictions of the individual life, of the singular community, of place and time, has magically fulfilled the basic human need for identification and permanence and has defeated the notions of isolation and transitoriness.

In a "Preliminary Note" and "A Note of Clarification" Rolando Hinojosa designates his "Sketches of the Valley" as self-contained and interrelated, claiming their own lives due to the strength of characters and situations. The role of the author is thus restricted from the outset.[26] Consequently, as in Hurston's "Anthology," the titles of the twenty sketches do not produce a common denominator.[27]

Looking for framing devices for the obviously heterogeneous materials, we encounter two collective scenes in end position, "Voices from the barrio" and "Round Table," suggesting an effort to impose order through atypical and/or functional situation. The search for communication and orientation reveals itself as a major theme, particularly after studying the first sketch of the series, "Braulio Tapia": The father of the bride relates his present situation to his own courting scene.[28] The chain of identification across the generations ends with his father-in-law, Braulio Tapia, because the speaker does not possess any further knowledge. His limitations are exposed in his unanswered final "Whom did don Braulio see at the threshold when he asked for his wife?"[29] The theme introduced here confirms Hinojosa's choice of the mode of presentation.

In the third sketch, "Roque Malacara," characters from "Braulio Tapia" recur. Roque Malacara, the former suitor, declares:

> My Tere gets tired and with good reason. We have a son, in addition to my father-in-law, we've also lost three little girls. My father-in-law was a good man. He loved to go fishing and he always found a way to take along his little namesake, Jehú. If people are reborn, I'd say that my son and his granddad are the same person.[30]

Here, the space of time is expanded to the next generation through the basic truths of human life, birth, death and, as in the previous sketch, through memory and identification compensating for loss.[31]

In the two final "estampas" we shall spot this Jehú in a courting scene among the "Voices from the barrio" and in "Round Table" as subject of the conversation of old men. It is significant that they are equally unable to reconstruct history beyond Braulio Tapia. So, the sequence of four generations and the final definition of the place, "Klail City, one of many towns in Belken County, Rio Grande Valley, Texas"[32] circumscribe the margins set for these sketches. Transgression is reserved for some citizens who by this act attain to eminent status, not necessarily for the community, but for individual narrators.[33]

Critics have reflected upon the fragmentation of this restricted world referring mainly to Hinojosa's use of the multiple point-of-view.[34] Articulation and dialogue occur in private situations like marriage, sickness and death requiring ceremony or ritual. The boundaries between the two spheres are not clearly marked as both public and private affairs can miraculously get out of hand[35] and subsequently, provoked misunderstandings and renewed verbalization.[36] Quite frequently the narrators try to show their utter surprise at life's consistencies and inconsistencies.[37] Very seldom do they find reliable stability.

A completely positive picture of human relations is drawn in the sketches dealing with don Víctor and Jehú, and in "Voices from the barrio."[38] In the collective scene the sounds of the younger and older generations are heard. But even there the community is portrayed as an accumulation of separate groups. The appraisal of this night as miraculous, as repetitive and a celebration of the people[39] gives this sketch a superior rank among the many scenes documenting the unreliability of experience. This construction stresses the desire of the people to save themselves some spheres of self-determination in a world closing in on them, also a longing for wholeness and order.[40]

How do the individual narrators and the characters introduced respond to these ambiguities? Like the Blacks in Hurston's "The Eatonville Anthology" many of the Chicanos demonstrate a remarkable pragmatism.[41] They all try to cope with their experience by verbalizing it, by fixing it and making their bewilderment known. Depending on the subject, their degree of personal involvement, their linguistic faculties and education, they develop individual varieties of tone and perspective.[42] But also common attitudes are established: Most of the time they ignore the Anglo and his civilization,[43] seeking their identity and their images in the Chicano world. Some try to relate to the Mexican Revolution or the victories won against the Texas Rangers;[44] others retreat to Chicano folklore, proverbial wisdom[45] and folk medicine.[46] Many insist on family ties and on giving people proper names and nicknames,[47] thus finding orientation in the community, even though these strategies might include some wishful thinking.

Without obvious interference of a superior narrator, the fragments gradually assemble into an expressive mosaic of one major segment of Belken County society. This seemingly self-propellent movement undoubtedly shuts out the nostalgic perspective and maintains the impression of a largely incoherent, unstable but vital reality including various strategies of response, efforts to keep up order and identity. Though the sketches generally evoke an atmosphere of simultaneousness[48] and not of sequence, the younger generation, represented by Jehú and Rafa, slowly but irresistibly moves to the forefront as subject of conversation, as persons pursuing social functions, and as speakers in their own right.[49] Their performances do not promise radical change as both of them seem to tolerate the "static heterogeneity" of this, in many ways, "restricted community."

In my comparison of the two cycles I am going to focus on the individual and the group, continuity and change, and the role of the narrator. Both texts largely define their characters through interpersonal relations. In Hinojosa's "Estampas del valle" the vicarious narrators constitute themselves as a group by their common urge to communicate through the verbalization of their own experience and that of others. Coherence between the individual encounters with reality is established in three collective scenes and through responses to the challenges of life with native strategies of the ethnic group, e.g. language and folklore.

In their actions and speeches the characters express a desire for independence *and* commitment, for individual *and* social identity according to the pressures they feel at the time. The enemy powers are never pinpointed, although we can conclude that the experience of isolation, insecurity, loss and the lack of perspective prompt them to retreat into the group. As they are not able to take advantage of its full potential, e.g. a new historical outlook, the characters do not build up a consistent group identity and very soon fall back into their individual selves. These shortcomings of Hurston's and Hinojosa's figures generate stasis as a predominant condition.

In both texts the group is primarily established in the reader's mind.[50] The characters never consciously define themselves as social beings. Other worlds beyond theirs occasionally forcing them to raise their flag as a community occur only marginally and are generally ignored. Hurston's narrator corrects these failures by cutting the individual encounters to size, to storytelling proportions so that they can become as much part of a communal tradition as the model animal tale.[51] Hinojosa also compensates for his narrators' limitations in "Voices from the barrio," though less visibly and comprehensively than Hurston.

By a process of transformation Hurston retrospectively liberates her characters and their stories from the conditions dominating the individual life, change and eventual death. This procedure asks for the capturing of a phase of small-town life, freezing it, making it disposable exactly as her characters prefer the collective, repetitive, stereotypical phenomena to experience continuity and familiarity. Whenever and wherever change occurs, Hinojosa's characters tend finally to accept it in view of their own ineffectuality. Hurston's figures frequently ignore or deny change in spite of their just-as-remarkable powers of acceptance. "The Eatonville Anthology" deliberately withdraws this place from the temporal process while Hinojosa leaves Belken County open for change and extinction, as his authorial retreat at the beginning implied. Of course, both techniques basically acknowledge the fact that the two traditional societies have been destroyed.

Contrary to this intended invisibility, Hinojosa is present in the selection of his material and, as telling, in his exclusion of many aspects of Chicano life.[52] Hinojosa and Hurston communicate with their audiences through the choice of framing devices, the sequence of the sketches, and the maintenance of the oral folk tone. Hurston seems to have less confidence in her reader, in the self-propellent energies of her characters and stories, in their qualities of endurance and the general cumulative effect of her sketches.[53] Both authors confirm their trust in language as a means of communication, stabilization and preservation.

Both "The Eatonville Anthology" and "Sketches of the Valley" were published in the initial, testing phases of their authors' career.[54] To establish this context, I shall briefly indicate the further development of the themes and techniques described in my analytical and comparative sections.

Zora Neale Hurston returned to the Eatonville setting in various stories, novels, her autobiography, a folklore documentation, a drama, and in some of her essays.[55] Her hometown provides a positive communal mood and morality, source of identification for herself, her characters, and a place where storytelling is practiced.[56] This locality is never exposed to change and development; sometimes even characters and situations recur in later works. The pervasive spirit of the place just receives different status among the structural elements of the texts. Only in *Their Eyes Were Watching God*, in her autobiography, and in *Mules and Men* do we occasionally get contrastive images of other places and social entities.[57] Some texts appear to be mere enlargements of the condensed Eatonville sketches, reversals of the folklore-in-the-making process.

The static quality of the place in the "Anthology" and in all her works seems to contradict Hurston's belief in vitality, in her well-developed sensitivity to contradictions as displayed in her essays and her autobiography.[58] These irritations can be dissipated when we take into consideration that the author assessed the values of Eatonville retrospectively, with a sense of loss, from the distance of her Northern experience. The term "anthology" in the title confirms this perspective.[59] Eatonville is conceived and presented as a reconstructed phase of Black communal life before the distortions through acculturation claimed their toll. For didactic purposes the illusion of permanence has to be established to re-activate the sources of communal ethnic identity. In some of her essays Hurston refused to let the racial question confine her life and art. She rather dedicated her fictional and documentary works to the re-vitalization and celebration of the heritage, putting it out of the reach of the majority culture.[60]

Rolando Hinojosa's re-creation of Chicano small-town life presents itself in a different context. His "Estampas" form part of his first larger work, the first building block of his *Klail City Death Trip Series*, to date comprising seven books.[61] In the subsequent titles the Chicano community loses its static quality as it is included into the historical process. Mobility and confrontation in Belken County cause the eventual destruction of traditional social structures.[62] We already recognized the fragmentary nature of "Estampas" as foreshadowing loss.[63]

In contrast to Hurston's method, Hinojosa chronicles the process of change in detail and does not merely imply it in a saving attempt. Step by step he focuses on more than one reality, various generations, slowly filling a large canvas with scenes of interdependence between individuals and various ethnic groups. In Hinojosa's work in progress the weaknesses and strengths of value systems are tested in a fluid, heterogeneous world producing both despair and endurance as extreme responses. Like human life Hinojosa's individuals and groups are on a permanent death trip.[64] Loss and death compete with vitality and creativity reflecting basic ambiguities of the human condition. This aspect gives the portrayal of the lost society of the "Estampas" struggling for survival a universal meaning. And after all, this world is still stimulating Hinojosa's creative energies as the "recasting and recreation in English"[65] of it in *The Valley* (1983) prove.

Hinojosa imitates the natural expansive mode of social orientation and the sequence of growth, stasis, destruction and reconstruction in the life of a community. Depicting a segment of Belken County society in its earliest memorable period, he invites the reader to re-assess the strengths and weaknesses of the traditional Chicano community. This is a procedure honoring the vitality and independence of his characters and readers, more democratic than Hurston's rather prescriptive method. Nevertheless, the two strategies of persuasion are used for the same ends, the establishment of community through the reconstruction and revitalization of the usable past.

Reconstructing small-town life is a theme not quite alien to American mainstream literature. I already mentioned Edgar Lee Masters' *Spoon River Anthology* (1915). The Midwest is also represented by Sherwood Anderson's *Winesburg, Ohio* (1919), the sequel *Poor White* (1920), and Sinclair Lewis' *Main Street* (1920). John Steinbeck contributed *Cannary Row* 91938) and Thornton Wilder built Grover's Corners in *Our Town* (1938). Moving South we could think of William Faulkner's Yoknapatawpha County and Larry McMurtry's Texas novels.[66] Most of these writers described their localities as threatened by change and eventual loss, and the majority of these works were published at a time when these worlds had already been destroyed. And it is also quite obvious that many of the authors wrote against the pervasive ideology among their contemporaries who either let the spirit of these communities fall into oblivion or tried to romanticize and mythologize it. Therefore Anderson, Masters, Lewis, Steinbeck, Wilder, and Faulkner share the intent of reconstruction, documentation, and re-interpretation, of making the past useful. These goals provide many roles for the writers, from historian, teacher, and social worker to outsider and nostalgic dreamer.

Considering these wide areas of correspondence between mainstream and minority, I still believe that themes like language, community, continuity, change and mobility, history, or endurance include special connotations in the works of ethnic writers. The trust in the power of the word as a tool to overcome powerlessness, forced muteness, is a first step towards identity and visibility as a group. For the minority leaving the community does not exclusively mean liberation from the confines of the small town, as for George Willard when he takes the train for Chicago at the end of *Winesburg, Ohio*, but a more ambiguous event, namely abandoning the protection granted by the community and moving into the domain of the enemy.[67] History and community have to be reconstructed and preserved in view of the deliberate denial, uprooting and destruction of alternative concepts as inferior by the majority civilization. This story of debasement forces ethnic writers to start from scratch, at the foundations of the communal building.

From the conserving function of the ethnic writers we should not conclude that they have to restrict themselves to traditional forms of writing. Interpreting the group heritage for a modern audience certainly asks for an innovative spirit who finds appropriate techniques of quote, integration and transformation. And retrieving the Black and Chicano past can be equally revolutionary in a mainstream culture with a shaky conceptional base. In many books a delicate balance between change and continuity is maintained as ethnic writers would not like to affirm an oppressive situation. On the other hand, the urge for stability does not imply a rejection of progress and civilization, a refusal to grow up. Zora Neale Hurston's "The Eatonville Anthology" and Rolando Hinojosa's "Estampas del valle" should be understood in the context of a recurrent trend to think small, to investigate the results of internal colonialism, to stress the varieties of the American and the human experience, and to revalue the sense of community.

[1] In Luis Leal, Fernando de Necochea, Francisco Lomelí, Roberto G. Trujillo, eds. *A Decade of Chicano Literature (1970–1979). Critical Essays and Bibliography* (Santa Barbara, 1982) pp. 9–17.
[2] *Ibid.* 12
[3] *Ibid.* 16
[4] *Ibid.* 17
[5] Quoted as EA from *The Messenger* 8,9 (September, 1926) pp. 332. Reprinted (with an incorrect publication date) in *The Norton Anthology of American Literature* II (New York, 1985²) pp. 1641–1651.
[6] "Estampas del valle/Sketches of the Valley," *Estampas del valle y otras obras* (Berkeley: Editorial Justa Publications, 1973). Quoted as EV.
[7] I am not at all interested in the discussion on the applicability of the term "novel" to Hinojosa's work. The same kind of argument started when Jean Toomer published *Cane* (1923) and Sherwood Anderson *Winesburg, Ohio* (1919). Unfortunately Hinojosa's explanations could not silence his critics. Cf. Juan Bruce-Novoa. *Chicano Authors. Inquiry by Interview.* (Austin, 1980), 59–60.
[8] (Urbana, Ill., 1977).
[9] *Ibid.*, 70.
[10] A collection of brief, confessional, explanatory or accusatory monologues of various authors, speaking up in the form of their epitaphs. Many of these statements are interrelated, the 244 former inhabitants of Spoon River talking about each other and themselves. The whole series of individual poems is loosely connected by a long poem by the editor, "The Spooniad" and an "Epilogue," a sort of play for voices by mythological figures.
[11] I. The Pleading Woman; II. Turpentine Love; III.; IV. Tippy; V. The Way of a Man with a Train; VI. Coon Taylor; VII. Village Fiction; VIII; IX; X; XI. Double-Shuffle; XII. The Head of the Nail; XIII. Pants and Cal'line; XIV. Section XIII remains fragmentary. The complete story can be found in Hurston's autobiography *Dust Tracks on a Road*, ed., by Robert E. Hemenway (New York, 1984²) pp. 22–25. The main character of Section XII, Daisy Taylor will recur in Hurston's and Langston Hughes' unpublished play "Mule Bone: A Comedy of Negro Life".

Cf. R.E. Hemenway. *Zora Neale Hurston. A Literary Biography*, pp. 184-154. The concluding Brer Rabbit story was also incorporated in Hurston's collection of Black folklore, *Mules and Men* (Philadelphia, 1935) pp. 145-146.

[12]Cf. R.E. Hemenway, *Zora Neale Hurston*, p. 70: "The fourteen parts have no thematic, structural, or imagistic relationship beyond their general identification with Eatonville in a bygone age."

[13]Cf.I. "Mrs. Tony Roberts is the pleading woman"; II. "Jim Merchant is always in good humor—even with his wife"; IV. "Sykes Jones' family all shoot craps." Even a statement like "Old Man Anderson lived seven or eight miles out in the country from Eatonville" not only refers to spatial but also psychic distance in this character. And a simple remark like "Mrs. Clarke is Joe Clarke's wife" (262) describes a basic situation.

[14]EA, 261

[15]*Ibid*. Section III includes striking parallels with motifs and themes in Jean Toomer's stories "Karfintha," "Becky" and "Blood-Burning Moon" from *Cane* (1923).

[16]EA, 262

[17]*Ibid*., 297. Cf. this story to Hinojosa's "Fira the Blond" in "Sketches of the Valley."

[18]Vague explanations are occasionally offered by referring to folk wisdom.

[19]Cf. e.g. EA, 297: "The town winked and talked. People don't make secrets of such things in villages . . . The town smiled in anticipation . . . So the town waited . . . " and 319: "He was hailed cheerily as he passed the sitters on the store porch . . . and set the porch to giggling and betting."

[20]EA, 262

[21]See "Double-Shuffle"

[22]Note the repetition of situations in IX and XI. Also the narrator's use of a mock jury trial in VII and elements of the tall tale in VII and VIII.

[23]Motifs of the animal tale very well relate to the preceding story, "Pants and Cal'line." For an introduction into the meanings of the Brer Rabbit tales see Maria Leach, ed. *Funk & Wagnalls Standard Dictionary of Folklore, Mythology and Legend* (New York, 1972) pp. 163 and the section "Animal Tales" in Langston Hughes and Arna Bontemps, eds. *The Book of Negro Folklore* (New York, 1958) pp. 1-30.

[24]Hurston's term as used in her autobiography and essays.

[25]EA, 332

[26]In the new version of this text, *The Valley* (1983), the author turns into the "complier"; the new titles of these notes are "On the Starting Blocks" and "A Word to the Wise (Guy)."

[27]Preliminary Note; a note of clarification; 1. Braulio Tapia; 2. Tere Noriega; 3. Roque Malacara; 4. Orphaned and Looking Forward; 5. My Cousins; 6. Harships of the Profession; 7. Learning the Profession; 8. Death Again; 9. Flora; 10. In the Pit with Bruno Cano; 11. Don Javier; 12. Emilio Tamez; 13. My Aunt Panchita; 14. Epigemio Salazar; 15. Fira the Blond; 16. Arturo Leyva; 17. Don Manuel Guzmán; 18. The Maestro; 19. Voices from the barrio; 20. Round Table.

Ten of these titles refer to individual names, two to family relations, five to individual situations worth telling, one to place, and the last two to conversational, collective scenes.

[28]Note the nearly identical vocabulary: "I say yes, we shake hands, and I let him in . . . Don Braulio says yes, shakes my hands and lets me come in" (40).
[29]EV, 40
[30]*Ibid.* 42
[31]Refers to loss of the family, friends or limbs. Cf. e.g. "Emilio Tamez" and "Don Javier."
[32]EV, 75
[33]Cf. "My Cousins" where El Mion "was granted a one way trip by the state government to the pen in Sugarland where, with diligence and great application, he trained himself to make license plates. This is a highly specialized profession but one not much in demand, as El Mion found out since he never got the opportunity to practise it after he completed schooling at Sugarland" (45). Also "Death Once Again": Don Víctor Pelaez' notes from the Mexican Revolution are introduced as texts for Jehú's reading practice but also explain his personal attachment to this new father figure. In "Don Manuel Guzman" the Mexican, Texas and Wyoming experience build up a considerable contrast to Guzmán's rather prosaic death. In "The Maestro" Rafa and don Genaro Castañeda "shared almost identical experiences: they passed like clouds that are dispersed by air and time" (71) though they went to two different wars, World War I and the Korean War.
[34]Cf. e.g. Rosaura Sánchez, "From Heterogeneity to Contradiction: Hinojosa's Novel" in José David Saldívar, ed. *The Rolando Hinojosa Reader. Essays Historical and Critical* (Houston: Arte Publico Press, 1985) pp. 76-100.
[35]As promised in the "Preliminary Note" Cf. e.g. "Don Javier" and "In the Pit with Bruno Cano." The grotesque situations created there by accident reach the proportions of Mark Twain's humor.
[36]Cf. e.g. "Don Manuel Guzmán."
[37]Typical examples can be found in "Braulio Tapia" "Orphaned and Looking Forward," "Don Javier" and "Epigemio Salazar."
[38]"Hardships of the Profession," "Learning the Profession" and "Death Once Again." These sketches, especially the first one of them, have the quality of Ernest Hemingway's Nick Adams stories. Other centers of stability are Tere of "Roque Malacara" and "Arturo Leyva" who functiions as a moral authority, and the altogether evil Salazar in "Epigemio Salazar" and "Arturo Leyva." In "Fira the Blond" Américo Paredes is quoted as an authority on the people of Jonesville. (cf. 67).
[39]EV, 73: "Now it's the *barrio*'s turn to sleep. In the *barrios* a lot is discussed and, miraculously, there's always something to talk about, night after night. The *barrios* can be called el Rebaje, el de las Conchas, el Cantarranas, el Rincón del Diablo, el Pueblo Mexicano—really, names don't matter much. What does count, as always, are the people." This statement is ironized in the following sketch when the old men of Klail City can only provide family trees as personal context for the people they discuss.

⁴⁰The notion of continuity and change is quite ambiguous. In "Tere Noriega" we hear the complaint: ". . . but I get tired of working and, if you really want to know, I get tired of the same old life" (41). In "My Cousins" a folk wisdom is quoted: "It seems that people don't like being confused," (49) another one in "Learning the Profession": "But according to Saint Thomas, force of habit forms its own rigorous code. . . " (49), and later, "Frankly, what was said wasn't anything new either and it might be that its greatest appeal was based on people's tastes which, and this is well-known, do not change without any warning" (49-50). Cf. also Don Javier's statement: ". . . not too many like her around anymore" (63) and the mood of loss in "Fira the Blond."

⁴¹Frequently shown in formulas like ". . . and that's it, you know?" (41), ". . . it's a known fact. . . " (45), "What else can you do?" (51), ". . . and that's that" (67), and ". . . but that's how it is and that's that" (71), signalling acceptance and an end of further elaboration. The formulas of consent and resignation resemble Kurt Vonnegut's "So it goes" in his *Slaughterhouse-Five* (1969). Charles M. Tatum comments on these stylistic means: ". . . the tone of resignation to a course of events over which the characters seem powerless to exert any control" (55) in "Contemporary Chicano Prose Fiction: Its Ties to Mexican Literature" in Francisco Jiménez, ed., *The Identification and Analysis of Chicano Literature* (New York: Bilingual Review Press, 1979) pp. 47-57.

⁴²In spite of these differences the general tone remains oral. One of the simplest forms of response is represented by "Tere Noriega": ". . . I'm what I am and what comes out, comes from the heart." This sketch competes with passages from "The Maestro" when Rafa obviously tries to imitate Don Genaro Castañeda's own account of his war experience. In spite of the fragmentation through multiplicity and rather bleak social conditions, an overall atmosphere of humor and good-naturedness is kept up.

⁴³The Anglo world is present in its wars, the daylight contrast to the night life of the barrio ("Voices from the Barrio") and in the merchandise at the candy vendor's of the circus (cf. "Learning the Profession", 50).

⁴⁴Cf. EV, 74

⁴⁵Not always very successfully as is shown in "Hardships of the Profession": ' "Yeah, like they say, we're in the same boat.' 'That's right, Jehú, we sure are. And just like Cuahutemoc says, eh? Do ya think I'm in bed of roses?' 'It was Moctezuma.' 'Was it? Okay. . . . ' " (47). The spirit of acceptance is very well expressed in the proverbial ". . . There's a little bit of everything in the Lord's vineyard." (45)

⁴⁶Cf. EV, 44: "Orphaned and Looking Forward" and "My Aunt Panchita". (65)

⁴⁷Cf. EV: ". . . it's a known fact that nicknames often take the place of everything else: first name, surname and even the character of the fortunate bearer." See also "Roque Malacara" and "The Maestro."

⁴⁸With only occasional flashbacks or foreshadowings. A typical example for the breaking up of chronological sequence is the end of "Death Once Again": ". . . I decided to say in Flora; once again death, once again an orphan, and once

more looking ahead" (56). Here, the title of this sketch and of "Orphaned and Looking Forward" are paraphrased. At the end of "Don Manuel Guzmán" his death is commented upon; in "Round Table" he "leaves to stroll through the streets of Klail City" (75).

[49]The author's presence can be observed in the associative linking of sketches, e.g. "Tere Noriega" and "Roque Malacara"; "Don Javier" and "Emilio Tamez"; "My Aunt Panchita" and "Epigemio Salazar." The author also guarantees that his narrators are granted the courtesy of being able to speak up without interference from others. See Yolanda Julia Broyles' article on "Hinojosa's *Klail City y sus alrededores*: Oral Culture and Print Culture" in José D. Saldívar, ed. *The Rolando Hinojosa Reader*, 109-132.

[50]Cf. Zora Neale Hurston, "Characteristics of Negro Expression" in Nancy Cunard, ed. *Negro. An Anthology* (New York, 1970; originally published 1934) pp. 24-31: "Negro folklore is not a thing of the past. It is still in the making. Its great variety shows the adaptability of the black man: nothing is too old or too new, domestic or foreign, high or low, for his use. . . the rabbit, the bear, the lion, the buzzard, the fox are culture heroes from the animal world. The rabbit is far in the lead of all the others and is blood brother to Jack" (27), and "It is said that Negroes keep nothing secret, that they have no reserve. This ought not to seem strange when one considers that we are an outdoor people accustomed to communal life. Add this to all-permeating drama and you have the explanation. . . discord is more natural than accord. If we accept the doctrine of the survival of the fittest there are more fighting honors than there are honors for other achievements. Humanity places premiums on all things necessary to its well-being, and a valiant and good fighter is valuable in any community. So why hide the light under a bushel?" (28)

[52]Hurston described an all-Black community! Cf. R.E. Hemenway, *Zora Neale Hurston*. . . , 11-12: "Eatonville, Florida, existed not as the 'black backside' of a white city, but as a self-governing, all-black town, proud and independent, living refutation of white claims that black inability for self-government necessitated the racist institutions of a Jim Crow South. Icorporated since 1886, Eatonville was, in Zora Hurston's words, 'a pure Negro town,' 'with charter, mayor, council, and town marshal; the only white folks were those who passed through.' "

[53]Cf. Günter H. Lenz, "Southern Exposures: The Urban Experience and the Re-Construction of Black Folk Culture and Community in the Works of Richard Wright and Zora Neale Hurston", *New York Folklore* 7/1-2 (1981) pp. 3-39: "Her work is characterized by a strong determination to transform everything into *one voice*, to reveal the unity manifested by her single narrative voice. . . "

[54]In 1926 Zora Neale Hurston had attained some popularity as the author of short stories and poems accepted mainly by the magazine *Opportunity*, the house organ of the *National Urban League*. One of her stories, "Spunk," had been reprinted in Alain Locke's path-breaking anthology *The New Negro* (1925).

[55]1924: "Drenched in Light" (short story); 1925: "Spunk" (short story); 1926: "Sweat" (short story); 1924: *Jonah's Gourd Vine* (novel); 1935: *Mules and*

Men (documentation); 1937: *Their Eyes Were Watching God* (novel); 1942: *Dust Tracks on a Road* (autobiography). Unpublished materials: "Eatonville When You Look at It" (essay); "Mule Bone: A Comedy of Negro Life" (play, written in cooperation with Langston Hughes).

[56]In *Their Eyes Were Watching God* the main character returns to Eatonville to tell her life story on Joe Clarke's front porch.

[57]In an unpublished series a comic verse, "The Book of Harlem", Hurston transferred some of "The Eatonville Anthology" techniques to another locality. Cf. R.E. Hemenway, *Zora Neale Hurston*. . . , 31.

[58]Cf. Robert E. Hemenway, "Introduction" to *Zora Neale Hur ston*. *Dust Tracks on a Road*, xix: "Zora constantly stresses in *Dust Tracks* her awareness of coexistent cultures. Even the process of assigning names demonstrates American biculturalism. Also Hurston's own comments in her autobiography: "So I sensed early, that the Negro race was not one band of heavenly love. There was stress and strain inside as well as out. Being black was not enough. It took more than a community of skin color to make your love come down on you. That was the beginning of my peace. . . Our lives are so diversified, internal attitudes so varied, appearances and capabilities so different, that there is no possible classification so catholic that it will cover us all, except my people! My people!" (234-235 and 237).

[59]Cf. *Anthology*: "The *Greek Anthology* of ca. 4100 epigrams and over 2000 other pieces, mostly in elegiac verse: amatory, dedicatory, sepulchral, epideictic, horatory, convivial, humorous. . . " (Joseph T. Shipley. *Dictionary of World Literature* Totowa, N.J., 1966). Edgar Lee Masters restricted the term to a collection of epitaphs, thus interpreting small-town life as a memorable but dead past.

[60]There is no doubt that this limitation can also be understood as a flaw, as an inability to keep up a more detached perspective.

[61]1973: *Estampas del valle y otras obras*; 1976: *Klail City y sus alrededores (Generaciones y semblanzas*, 1977); 1978: *Korean Love Songs*; 1981: *Mi querido Rafa*; 1982: *Rites and Witnesses*; 1985: *Partners in Crime*; 1986: *Claros Varones de Belken*; 1987: *Klail City*.

[62]Cf. Rosaura Sánchez' statement: ". . . it is only in the last two books that the destruction of the Valley idyll is complete and that social contradictions beyond ethnicity become manifest. The novel's movement from heterogeneity to contradiction will be analyzed in terms of the text's time-space framework and its intertextuality, with a focus on the novel's dialogue with history." ("From Heterogeneity to Contradiction: Hinojosa's Novel," in J. D. Saldivar, ed. *The Rolando Hinojosa Reader*, 76-100) p. 77.

[63]But the titles of Hinojosa's books still stress collectivity: "The very titles of Hinojosa's novels convey collectivity: *Klail City y sus alrededores* and *Generaciones y semblanzas*. These collective nouns in the plural at once span numerous time (generations), spaces (Klail City y sus alrededores) and agents (semblanzas). Both of Hinojosa's titles imply a broad scope, unlike the scores of Chicano titles which reveal a reduced, particularistic, often individualistic, primary focus: *Bar-

rio Boy; Autobiography of a Brown Buffalo; Bless Me, Ultima; . . . *y no se lo tragó la tierra; Pocho.* Where these works do include community, it is filtered through the experiences of the protagonist." (110) (Yolanda Julia Broyles, "Hinojosa's *Klail City y sus alrededores*: Oral Culture and Print Culture," in J.D. Saldívar, ed. *The Rolando Hinojosa Reader*, 109-132).

[64] Hinojosa's switch from Spanish to English in *Korean Love Songs, Rites and Witnesses, Partners in Crime,* and even in *The Valley* closely relates to the theme of destruction and loss.

[65] José David Saldívar, "Rolando Hinojosa's *Klail City Death Trip*: A Critical Introduction," in *The Rolando Hinojosa Reader*, 44-63; p. 47.

[66] *Horseman, Pass By* (1961); *Leaving Cheyenne* (1963); *The Last Picture Show* (1966); *Moving On* (1970) also Dylan Thomas *Under Milk Wood* (1954) and Gabriel García Márquez' Macondo novels.

[67] Cf. Nash Candelaria's *Memories of the Alhambra* (1977) and Rudolfo Anaya's *Heart of Aztlán* (1967); N. Scott Momaday's *House Made of Dawn* (1968) and Leslie M. Silko's *Ceremony* (1977); Richard Wright's *Native Son* (1940) and Jean Toomer's *Cane* (1923). In Toomer's book the movement from rural Georgia, the birthplace of the communal tradition, in Section One to Washington, D.C. in Section Two, and the attempt of an uprooted Black intellectual to return to Georgia in Section Three comprises most of the themes treated by the other ethnic writers. Unfortunately Toomer did not continue his writer's career after *Cane* and did not demonstrate how his materials could be further developed and adapted to the historical process. Cf. Heiner Bus, "Jean Toomer and the Black Heritage," in Günter H. Lenz, ed. *History and Tradition in Afro-American Culture* (Frankfurt, 1984) pp. 56-83.

> history remains
> a silent poet
> and class struggles
> its verb on earth.

Myth, Identity and Struggle in Three Chicano Novels:
Aztlán . . . Anaya, Méndez and Acosta

Alurista
California State University at San Luis Obispo

Mexicans became de facto U.S. citizens through the Guadalupe Hidalgo Treaty which ceded half of northern Mexico to the United States in 1848. Such an event in no way diminished the relationship which these people maintained with Mexico and things Mexican.[1] In fact, if one could speak of their steady acculturation and assimilation into North American culture, one could, on the other hand, readily point out the inumerable ways through which Mexicans in the U.S. tried—often successfully—to preserve their cultural integrity.[2] The history of the "American Southwest" between 1848 and 1969 reveals the indelible contributions to the culture and the industrial coming of age of the territory which Mexicans once called their homeland. It also reveals the methodical exploitation and mistreatment of generations of Mexicans—both native and immigrated—to the point of forcing them into anomic behavior, a self-defeating identity crisis, and the social alienation predicated on a state founded on racial, sexual, ethnic and class oppression.

While the subordination of Mexican workers escalated immediately following the American occupation of northern Mexico, now referred to as "the southwestern United States," one should note that numerous revolts sought to regain some of the dignity the loss of land, language and culture had occasioned. Some political and material gains were sometimes achieved, and Chicano sociologists and labor historians have contributed significantly in this research area.[3] This paper will also focus on "struggle," but of a very different nature—though inextricably connected with material, dialectical, class struggle—and that is: the desire and struggle of U.S. Mexicans, of Chicanos, to think or, better yet, *rethink* themselves as one, as whole, and as a meaningful people on earth. *How* this struggle and desire is manifest in three contemporary Chicano narratives which make use of myth as the unifying force in the psyche of the Chicano characters in their novelistic production constitutes the primary and central concern of this critical inquiry. The myth, common to all three novels, which this study will unveil, is *Aztlán*. The novels to be examined are: 1) *Peregrinos de Aztlán (Pilgrims of Aztlán)* by Miguel Méndez; 2) *The Revolt of the Cockroach People* by Oscar Z. Acosta; and, 3) *Heart of Aztlán* by Rudolfo Anaya.

Before proceeding to an analysis of each text it may be appropriate to discuss briefly "myth," particularly as it is to be distinguished from "fantasy." Fantasy is, more often than not, the product of an individual mind that chooses to see the world, the real, through a non-ordinary set of manufactured, that is to say, made-up conditions. Fantasy artificially constructs a world which in fact becomes a form, a way of escaping the real one. Fantasy may project itself into the future and, in fact, predict possible developments in the concrete world (such is the case of Jules Verne's science fiction) so that what is clearly false and non-existent at a given point in historical timespace can, with the inevitable passage of time in the same or different space, become a reality, a palpable and veritable event or thing.

Myth, on the other hand, is always the product of not only more than one mind, but, in fact, of several generations who share a particular space over a significant period of time. Myth has, if obscure more often than not, a historical consensus. Functionally, it differs from fantasy in that myth connects a people more solidly with their timespace; instead of distancing one from the real, myth explains and gives significance to the individual's life within a larger, often cosmic, always generationally social, context. Myth has historically been the fabric with which civilizations, that is to say, large social formations, were bound together as in a covenant. Consensus, collective consensus, is the key to the understanding of myth. At the very core of both fantasy and myth resides desire. Desire in fantasy results in the fulfillment, vicarious or symbolic, of otherwise, in the real world, impossible objectives and it often leads to the development of new options or ideas that may be practicable in the future. In myth, desire results in the reunion of the individual with the collective species being as well as the natural and cosmic world within which one lives; the terms religion and yoga, for example, mean just that: to reunite, to be one with the otherness.[4]

The myth upon which the three novels, here to be examined, are based is a myth of origin. The myth of Aztlán has at least three traditions in distinct historical periods. For the purposes of this study, I will call the first "The Pre-Mexica" version.

The Pre-Mexica version dates back to the arrival of the first settlers of what is today known as Mexico, which could be as far back as 19,000 B.C.[5] In this version of the myth, Aztlán is situated east of the present day peninsula of Yucatan and the Gulf of Mexico. It is thought to be an island, now lost in the Atlantic Ocean, where an advanced civilization, the Chanes (which means the "people of the snake" in Mayan) established the center of their civilization, which extended itself east to India and Egypt and west to Mexico, Yucatan and Central America.

The second version, the Mexica's Aztlán, was the product of the theocratic militarism which Tlacaelel, an advisor to three Aztec/Mexica rulers, crafted to be the motherland of the Mexica. It was crafted for *only* the Mexica, and not the whole of the people populating Mexico at the time of their arrival to mesoamerica and the central valley of Mexico during the later quarter of the first millenium after Christ and a half century before the arrival of the Spaniards.[6] Motecuhzoma Ilhuicamina actually sent an expedition to the north of Tenochtitlan (present day Mexico City) searching for vestiges of the Mexica motherland: Aztlán. This version would have located the center of the geographical Aztlán somewhere around the four corners area in the southwestern United States. The purpose of the journey was, clearly, to legitimize the power which the Mexicas had come to wield by the fourteenth century A.D. This Aztlán was also believed to be the source, the origin of the Mexica lineage.

The third version of reference to Aztlán, the Chicano version, is elaborated in "The Spiritual Plan of Aztlán" drafted and legitimized by the delegates to the first national Chicano youth conference held in Denver, Colorado, during March of 1969. Here, again, we find that Aztlán is used as a metaphor which unifies the various delegations from all over the United States into one nationalist body. Aztlán, in this case, is referred to as being more than a geographical location when the plan states at its closure: "We are Aztlán."[7] Here the myth assumes a different role. Aztlán is no longer just an origin, a source, a motherland, a testimony to an ancient heritage and tradition. Aztlán has become a mission and a state of mind, a way of facing contemporary reality and social conditions. The plan speaks of reclaiming that which once belonged to its original inhabitants: the fruits and the wealth of the land which its heirs still work to date. Rightful ownership is not established, however, on the basis of lineage, but rather on the basis of "those who work it." "Borders," geographical boundaries, are not to be drawn so that Aztlán in this case may be the actual equivalent to the American continent and its inhabitants.[8] The novels which this study proposes to examine were all written after 1969, and all three of them make reference to both the Mexica and the Chicano version of the myth; none of them address the legendary Aztlán, Aztlán, Atlantis, of the Pre-Mexica, Mayan version. At this point we shall focus on the work of Rudolfo Anaya: *Heart of Aztlán* (1976). We shall then proceed with Miguel Mendez: *Pilgrims of Aztlán*, (1974), then to finalize this inquiry with Oscar Z. Acosta's work: *The Revolt of the Cockroach People* (1973).

Heart of Aztlán is a novel set in the forties. The story is linear and simple: a Chicano family leaves their rural home in Guadalupe, New Mexico, to search for work and a new lease on life in Albuquerque. This move is the cause of great pain to the father, principally, who has to sell his land in order to make the move. Without land, Clemente Chávez (the protagonist of the novel), feels alienated, rootless and without a clear identity or destiny. The work that he finds with the Santa Fe railroad soon turns sour because of a much-needed strike for better wages and working conditions. The family itself begins to suffer from the disintegrating influence of the city; his children begin to lose the traditional respect accorded parents in a Chicano, New Mexican rural setting. Crispin, a blind poet who possesses a "magical blue guitar," along with a witch who possesses a "magical black stone," become the sources of new hope for Clemente, his family and his people by rekindling the myth of Aztlán as an original source of power and new faith.

Anaya, more so than the other two authors examined here, uses myth as a healing power capable of restoring self-respect, self-worth, and self-determination. When Clemente finds himself at the end of his wits and faces the total destruction of his self concept, Crispin rescues him from a frozen death in an alley and introduces him to the legend of Aztlán. The workers on strike find themselves hopeless and without a leader. Crispin feels that Clemente is the chosen one to receive the power of the myth and then to transfer it, convert it into new strength for his people; Clemente speaks:

> "Por Dios Santoí . . . that is what I need to live! I will search for those signs, I will find that magic heart of our land about which you whisper [the heart of Aztlán], and I will wrestle from it the holy power to help my people . . . I don't know if this is an insanity that possesses me, but at least it has a purpose, I feel that purpose!" (Heart: 122-23)

Myth, in this context, is magical and can help Clemente in his struggle to rethink, to redefine himself and his people. The myth of Aztlán is a powerful source for the development of a new, self-affirming identity.

Clemente is told that the "heart of Aztlán" was located somewhere around Albuquerque and the Sandia mountains. The founders of the legendary Aztlán were asked to leave it in order to journey south to establish a great civilization (that of the Mexicas) but were told that they would journey back in the future in order to reclaim its original splendor. Reference is made here to the Mexica and the Chicano version of the myth where Aztlán is an original motherland, a mission to be accomplished and a power to be harnessed. Anaya has captured in this novel the most positive aspects that a myth can present to a people in need of rediscovering their worth and a reason to live and struggle for. While it is clear that the material conditions suffered by the striking workers is sufficient cause for their material struggle, it is also clear that a spiritual vacuum has to be filled by something other than the traditional Catholic faith which promises the Kindgom of Heaven for the poor and the meek. Aztlán is the myth, the force, the psychic construct that can and, at least in the novel, indeed, fill the spiritual (i.e., psychological) void experienced by Clemente, his family, and the striking workers. This myth offers some relief on earth and it calls for social and political struggle as opposed to calling for penance, patience and blind faith for a better world in the afterlife. At one point Clemente exclaims, "I am Aztlán" so that the mythical place is transformed into a state of being, after which he accepts the leading role amongst the strikers. At the end of the novel the people have resolved to struggle and Clemente leads them:

> Crispin strummed a tune of liberation on the blue guitar. The people began to move, marching to a *new* step, singing the songs of the revolution which would *create their destiny*. Around the perimeter of the shops armed guards fingered their rifles nervously. The dogs they held on leashes growled uneasily. They could smell fear, but they were not trained to deal with the burning force that came singing up the barrio street. In the dark, cold night the blaring sirens announced the mobilization of another force at the barricades, but the people did not hesitate. "Adelante!" they shouted without fear. (Heart: 208-9)

The rekindling of an old myth, at least in this novel, results in a new faith, in a new self concept and courage to be, bridging the 1930's with the 50's and the 70's.

Mendez addresses Aztlán as a land to which the ancestors of the ancient Mexicas now return, as undocumented workers.

> Del sur iban, a la inversa de sus antepasados, en unaperegrinación sin sacerdotes ni profetas, arrastrando una historia sin ningún mérito para el

> que llegara a contarla, por lo vulgar y repetido de su tragedia. Sin embargo, unepisodio de la vida de Ramagacha, mucho tiempo después de sucedido, sirvió de cita a un hombre que conversaba en grupo, palmote ndo los zancudos enrabiados, que en centenare sembraban de ronchas y comezón las pieles sudorosas. (Peregrinos: 64)

Aztlán for Mendez is not mythical utopia or even the new society that the heirs of the ancients are to bring to its traditional glory. Aztlán is the territory occupied by the norteamericanos *and* the capitalist Mexicanos on the borderland between the U.S. and Mexico; it is a place of toil and misery for those who have recently returned. And, for those who have been in the territory for generations, it is a place where their labor is exploited and their dignity stripped away on the basis of cultural, racial and economic differences. The novelistic production of Mendez focuses on the alienation which abounds in a land of wealth, a wealth that, even though produced by a majority working class, is enjoyed only by a handful. The silent poet, history, is not silent in the Mendez novel at all, but is in fact ever present. Dialogical class discourse in *Peregrinos de Aztlán* is most deliberately codified through the meticulous characterization of the various personages which populate his novel. Myth, here, conversely becomes the absent cause, the origin lost which history and concrete social conditions will *not* allow its protagonist to retrieve as a source of hope, or even traditional pride. There is no narrative space allotted to the myth of Aztlán becoming a state of mind or a source of consciousness. Aztlán, for Mendez, is at best a nationalist ideal to be sought and fought for by a new generation yet to come. A generation that, in his own terms, will not be willing to tolerate the kind of institutionalized ethnocentrism, racism and class oppression to which Mexicans, Native Americans, *and* other Third World people are subjected to in the United States. At worst, Aztlán is a long lost legend that has become a nightmare embodied and disguised in the so-called "American Dream."

The Revolt of the Cockroach People by Oscar Z. Acosta was the first novel to be published which made reference to the myth. If for Anaya Aztlán is a healing myth and for Mendez a future ideal, Aztlán is a contemporary war cry for Acosta.

> Christmas Day, seven hours after the arrest of the St. Basil Twenty-One, we returned, this time without picket signs or candles. I am still numb, grim from my conversation with Stonewall. While the Faithful inside pray and count their beads, we march silently in front of the church and demand the release of our prisoners.

The media turn out in full force. Chicanos have not fought inside a temple since the Spanish conquistadores invaded the shrines of Huitzilopochtli in the Valley of Mexico. We make headlines without the assistance of Stonewall and his liberal white connections. McIntyre heaps it on us. We are the rabble at the foot of the cross, calling for the death of Christ. We are agents of the devil and communists to boot.

"Actually, we're Jewish underground," I say with a straight face. The man taping the conversation has told me he is from the biggest newspaper in Tel Aviv. He doesn't smile.

A team with cameras tells us they are making a film in America. They are from Berlin and want me to explain the purpose of our demonstration. I tell them that the Church and government have combined to exterminate us. "We are the Jews of Nazi America," I tell the people of Berlin.

A reporter from LIFE wants to know if any of our members are affiliated with radicals. How do I answer the charges of the Cardinal and the Chief of Police?

"Well . . . yes, I belong to some violent organizations,"
I say.

"Is this for publication?"

"You can tell the whole world, mister."

"Well. . . ?"

"I'm an American citizen. . . . Nixon is my leader." (Revolt: 78-79)

Acosta's novel best exemplifies the "Chicano version" of the myth though he makes no specific reference to it. The "revolt" which he addresses in his narrative clearly implies it. Here, again as with Mendez, we find a narrative where class discourse and history, far from being an absent cause—the silent presence which speaks between the lines—is the central dialogical strategy of his literary production. His novel is written in what has come to be called a "gonzo" style where the author is a participant observer in the world of events which he narrates. Acosta focuses on the Chicano revolt in Los Angeles, California, between 1968-70, a period during which thousands of Chicanos mobilized publicly to assert their self-determinant presence in the U.S. It is during this period that Aztlán becomes *the* metaphor which best codifies the nationalist Chicano fervor of the sixties. Acosta mediates the alienation of the days of the "revolt" through mythic, nonordinary mental states and a stark and cynical irony. Aztlán, in Acosta's narrative code, though not enunciated significantly, is evoked as a force, the force of history and class, sexual and cultural contradictions that prevail during the social space between the sixties and the eighties.

Anaya uses myth as a "healer," whereas Mendez sees myth as a restructuring agent, and Acosta renders myth as a revolutionary war cry. All three codify Aztlán as borderless and belonging to those who work, who toil for the wealth that, presently, others who own the means of production enjoy. Aztlán is a cry for struggle, redefinition, and self-determination; it abhors war, misery and the total annihilation of the human species in any of the novels here examined. Aztlán is positioned as an origin and the promise of a future possibility for a more humane social formation.

> P.S. I was just one of a bunch of Cockroaches that helped start a revolution to burn down a stinking world. And no matter what kind of end this is, I'll still play with matches. (Revolt: 257-58)

[1]While there are many works on the subject I would recommend two general works for a panoramic introduction of the history and relationship of the "borderland" Chicano/Mexican connection. *North of Mexico* by Carey McWilliams and *Occupied America* by Rudy Acuña.

[2]Here again the work of numerous scholars in the history and sociology of Mexicans in the U.S. should be examined for a thorough discussion on the subject. A brief listing follows: *The Mexican-American People* by Grebler, More and Guzman; *A Documentary History of Mexican-Americans* by Wayne Moquin; *Mexican-Americans in the U.S.* by John H. Burma; *Introduction to Chicano Studies* by Duran and Bernard (First and Second Editions/ Articles vary); *Chicano Manifesto* by Armando Rendon; *La Otra Cara de México* by Carlos Mousivais and David Maciel.

[3]The work of professor Dr. Juan Gómez-Quiñonez, precursor and "father" of Chicano labor history research, is a must (many of his students have contributed significantly as well: Luis Arroyo, David Weber, Emilio Zamora, Victor N. Cisneros, et al). *Orígenes del Movimiento Obrero Chicano* by Juan Gómez-Quiñonez and Luis Leobardo Arroyo as well as *Las ideas políticas de Ricardo Flores Magon* by Juan Gómez-Quiñonez. Also look up *Race and Class in the Southwest* by Mario Barrera.

[4]The discourse on myth to be found throughout the works of Mircea Eliade and Claude Levi-Strauss are particularly relevant to our discussion of the role and function of myth in the development of large social formations and what they consider to be their "civilized" concensus.

⁵While the antiquity of the Maya-Itzae (The "old" Maya), the Olmecs and the Toltecs is far from being irrevocably settled by anthropologists or archeologists do look up *Queen Moo, the Maya and Atlantis* for a linguist's approach to the question of antiquity and translantic contact; this book is authored by Augustus Le Plongeon.

⁶*Los Antiguos Mexicanos* and *Aztec Thought and Culture* by Miguel Leon-Portilla are essential works for an introduction to the study of the theocratic militarism of the Mexicas/Aztecs.

⁷Armando Rendon, in his *Chicano Manifesto,* includes a number of "declarations of independence" in an appendix to his text. "El plan espiritual de Aztlán" is included there and a discussion of it is found in chapters 1-15.

⁸Rendon, Armando. Ibid. Appendix.

Code-Switching as Metaphor in Chicano Poetry

Cordelia Candelaria
University of Colorado at Boulder

The poetic imagination is as persistent as a cactus flower. Despite the awesome strength of the forces that challenge it, that imagination persists in expressing its specific truths and impressions clearly visible in Chicano poetry, a body of the literature of the Americas that has lived, and even flourished, quietly for over a century. Not only has Chicano poetry suffered the blistering hostility of a U.S. literary tradition that would deny the legitimacy of non-British origin, non-English language forms, it also has had to endure the indifference of a publishing industry content to promote literature patterned only in recognizable Yankee forms, however esoteric and avant-grade they might be. But though Mexican American poets and their audiences may be seen as victims of a harsh literary environment, Chicano poetry itself is neither victim nor loser. It is, rather, a testament to *chicanismo*—to its vast and multifold riches as well as to its dynamic and irrepressible creativity.

The attributes resonate with special strength and timbre in the language of Chicano poetry, particularly in its multilingualism, that polyphonic code of sound and sense which ramifies out of the least six different language systems. For background reference, they are:

1. Standard edited American English.
2. English slang (regional dialects and vernaculars including varieties of Black English).
3. Standard Spanish.
4. Dialectal Spanish (regional vernaculars including caló).
5. English/Spanish or Spanish/English blends of bilingualism.
6. An amalgam of pre-American indigenous languages, mostly noun forms from Nahuatl and Mayan.

Moreover, Chicano poetry manifests a variety of combinations of these six systems so that a given poem, like Chicano bilingual speech, might disclose yet another, different combination form, and so on. *The point is that the phonological, morphological, syntactic, and semantic possibilities of Chicano poetry are astonishingly flexible and extensive.*

To demonstrate one aspect of these remarkable possibilities this paper examines one linguistic area of Chicano poetry, its code-switching. My thesis is that code-switching in Chicano poetry is emblematic of theme. That is, specific transition itself—the discrete speech act of changing from one language to another and back again—conveys meaning quite apart from the lexical meanings denoted or the symbolic meanings connoted by the surface language forms. The thesis is best argued through application, for which I have chosen a well-known poem by Alurista and a less familiar but more recent piece by Carmen Tafolla. These texts were selected to illustrate some of the different kinds of code-switching found in Chicano poetry. In Alurista's piece, the code-switching presents two languages in separate syntactic units, each operating independent of the other, whereas Tafolla's intermixes two languages interdependently within a syntactic unit. Scholars have described these two types as, respectively, *bilingual* and *interlingual* (Bruce-Novoa, 1982, 226).

"address"

address
occupation
age
marital status
—perdone. . .
yo me llamo pedro
telephone
height
hobbies
previous employers
—perdone. . .
yo me llamo pedro
pedro ortega
zip code
i. d. number
classification
—perdone mi padre era
el señor ortega
(a veces don josé)
race

Alurista (Floricanto, 1971)

Written in plain, elemental language, "address" lacks the figurative multiplicity typical of Alurista's best known style with its pervasive use of pre-American motifs, images of *mestizaje*, and references to the Chicano Movement. Here, the simplicity of the diction and its many repetitions achieve a formulaic minimalism that underscores the poem's thematic focus on the failure of communication in a bureaucratic society. To convey his theme Alurista relies on code-switching to contrast the two languages and, by extension, the cultures they represent. For instance, the English language portion consists almost entirely of nouns—no verbs, articles or any trace of grammatical syntax—whereas the Spanish, though given fewer lines, evinces a grammatical completeness that underscores its semantics and thus heightens the difference between idioms, a difference extending far beyond language.

Like other Phase II Chicano poems (Candelaria, 1986, 71), "address" deals with the insensitivity of a modern bureaucracy which has become impersonal as the machine-produced forms it uses to spindle and mutilate the people it is supposed to serve. On one level the poem duplicates the attempted communication between a Mexican (or Chicano) and a bureaucrat so inured to the surrounding Orwellian routine that s/he resembles a machine. Through metonymy, however, the poem demonstrates on another level the sterile impersonality of Yankee culture in its dominance over ethnic minorities. Pedro Ortega, a metonym for all colonized *raza*, wishes to identify by reference to his name, his father, and his father's respectability. But his inquisitor perceives him solely in terms of external variables associated with an easily categorized, superficial *identification*. As a result, the dialogue is at best parallel, not interactive, and they fail to communicate.

Yet having asserted the foregoing in discussing the poem's theme, one must ask, WHY IS THIS SO? WHERE IN THE TEXT DOES ONE PROVE IT? Certainly nothing in the English words themselves denote cultural polarity of values. Perhaps Pedro Ortega is meant to be seen as deranged and absurdly talking to himself while completing a form of some sort. To take such an alternative reading seriously, however, would be to seriously undermine the poem's considerable merit. Instead, we must conclude that the overall meaning depends directly on the English to Spanish code-switching which occurs four times in the available linguistic choices and permits him to allude to both the dominant Anglo and the minority Chicano cultures efficiently. Thus, despite its brevity and *because of* the code-switching, "address" manages to reflect a considerable range of U.S. society. Especially effective is the final shift which carefully isolates "race" in the last line to draw dramatic attention to the fundamental significance of race and racism in U.S. American society. Its isolation confirms what the rest of the poem implies—that despite the strengths and richnesses of his culture, Señor Ortega is precluded from socioeconomic opportunities primarily because of his race, which also precludes meaningful interaction with either the bureaucracy or the dominant culture that produced it.

"Woman-Hole"

Some say there is a
vacuum—a black hole—
in the center of womanhood
that swallows countless
secrets and has strange
powers

Yo no sé de'sas cosas
solo sé que the
black echo is music
is sister of sunlight
and from it
crece
vida.

Carmen Tafolla (*Revista Chicano-Riqueña*, 1983)

The first stanza of Tafolla's poem sets up the straw man of patriarchal tradition regarding the reputed eternal mystery of women and the mystique of femininity. Employing paradox to draw attention to the conflicting perceptions of women characteristic of that tradition, Tafolla exposes the bizarre contradictions within those perceptions. For example, there is paradox in her title, which is at once a crude reference to a part of female physiology and also an emblem of the romanticization of "Woman" throughout the ages. There is paradox, too, in the yoking of "vacuum" (i.e., "a black hole" signifying nothingness) with the capacity (i.e., somethingness) to consume "countless secrets" arising out of the "strange powers." The one would seem to cancel the other. Extending the paradox to the second stanza, the poet introduces an outwardly humble "yo" who asserts ignorance of the conceptualizations just described, but who then immediately proceeds to exhibit enough sophistication to indulge in synesthetic and oxymoronic comparisons. By reducing the first stanza's concepts to mere "cosas," the speaker cleverly reverses history's reductive objectification of women, whether on pedestal or pillory, throughout the centuries. Tafolla then offers her own "woman-hole" metaphors in the synthesthetic of sound ("echo") and sight ("sunlight") and the oxymoron of darkness ("black") being "sister" to daughter's ("sunlight"). She then switches again to Spanish in the concluding lines which affirm the literal fact that "from it/ crece/ vida." Also contributing to the metaphor is the poem's print pattern suggestive of womb and vagina as well as the hourglass figure of male fantasy against which the female form has traditionally been measured. Through these techniques the poet makes concrete the idea that self-definition by women is a requisite prelude to self-discovery of our literal worth.

Crucial to this reading of "Woman-Hole" is a thematic interpretation of its code-switching, for it alone accounts for the distinct separation of the speaker from those who "say there is a vacuum . . . in the center of womanhood." The interlingualism in stanza two emphasizes the speaker's separate identity as an individual woman whose self-perception derives from such primal elements as music and sunlight. (Parenthetically, these elements are themselves symbols of two fundamental kinds of life, the creative and the procreative.) The shift to an interlingual idiom distances the speaker and, logically, all her "sister [s]" from the standard canons accountable for the sexist language and thought which are the implicit subjects of stanza one. Without the intermixing of languages the poem might still aptly capture the contradictions within the patriarchal objectification of estrangement from the civilization that produced her.

Accordingly, Tafolla's code-switching brings to the foreground a contrast between what Mircea Eliade describes as the diurnal and the nocturnal modes of mind—that is, the rationality of conscious thought vs. the intuition of subconscious insight (Eliade, 1959). According to Eliade, the epistemological goal is a dynamic balance between modes to account inclusively for the wide variety of experience and discourse in any age. Both Tafolla and Alurista achieve, I believe, that kind of dynamic inclusivity. Tafolla suggests the strict rationality of the diurnal mode in her first stanza's scientific "vacuum" and "black hole," but she reverses it to pseudo-science in the last three lines of that stanza. The reversal establishes a context for the next stanza's interlingual switch to the nocturnal mode with its metaphorical comparison which derives from the intuitive artistry of the subconscious. A similar polarity appears in Alurista's "address." The English language lines capture the cold sterility of a totally dehumanized diurnal rationality which is incapable of engaging the subjective, intuitive faculties of emotion and familial identity. Oppositely, the

Spanish lines suggest the fuller, more holistic nocturnal mode reaching back to a more primal humanistic tradition. The code-switching in both poems makes the contrast of perspective particularly salient.

The skin of language is the only universally shared system that can cover every facet of multitudinous experience. Language is the only skin large enough to be shared, but when we try to objectify it for empirical analysis the result is much like Fausto Tejada's experience in *The Road to Tamazunchale* when he peels off his his skin and finds that its mass is so small he can place it in the palm of his hand. The narrow structuralist study of language sometimes yields about as much as Fausto's skin: a palm-full of alphabet representing a taxonomy of phonemes that constitute the skin of communication. But language is vastly, complexly more than the skin itself. It is simultaneously the externalization of experience, both private and shared, past and present, actual and imagined, while it is also what defines and records that experience. Hence, to comprehend the multilayered nature of experience captured in Chicano poetry requires that any analysis of the poetry be attentive to its linguistic categories.

In this paper I have sought to apply such attention to one linguistic aspect of two poems to demonstrate the thematic centrality of code-switching in itself and quite apart from other linguistic elements and categories. These titles join countless others in illustrating that code-switching in Chicano poetry, whether bilingual or interlingual, (a) enriches the linguistic repertoire, (b) alludes to culture, (c) reflects the social matrix, (d) asserts an ethnocultural autonomy, and (e) manifests the dichotomy of values implicit in the diurnal vs. the nocturnal modes of mind. Consequently, like other metaphors, the act of code-switching must be comprehended not only as a linguistic vehicle for literary expression but as a multiplicitous symbolic element of the text.

Alurista. *Floricanto en Aztlán*. Los Angeles: UCLA Chicano Studies Research Program, 1971.

_____*Return: Alurista Poems Collected and New*, Gary Keller, ed. Ypsilanti, Michigan: Bilingual Press/Editorial Bilingüe, 1982.

Bruce-Novoa, Juan. *Chicano Poetry: A Response to Chaos*. Austin: University of Texas Press, 1982.

Candelaria, Cordelia. *Chicano Poetry, A Critical Introduction*. Westport,

Connecticut: Greenwood Press, 1986.

———*Ojo de la Cueva/Cave Springs*. Colorado Springs, Colorado: Maize Press, 1984.

Eliade, Mircea. *The Sacred and the Profane*. New York: Harper Torchbooks, 1959.

Gumperz, John J. and Dell Hymes, eds. *Directions in Sociolinguistics*. New York: Holt, Rinehart and Winston, 1972.

Gunn, Giles. *The Interpretation of Otherness: Literature, Religion and the American Imagination*. New York: Oxford University Press, 1979.

Martínez, Julio A. and Francisco A. Lomelí, eds. *Chicano Literature: A Reference Guide*. Westport, Connecticut: Greenwood Press, 1985.

Tafolla, Carmen, et al. *Get Your Tortillas Together*. San Antonio, Texas: S/A Publications, 1976.

Vigil, Evangelina, ed. *Woman of Her Word: Hispanic Women Write*, *Revista Chicano-Riqueña*, 11:3-4 (1983).

Homosexuality and the Chicano Novel

Bruce-Novoa
Trinity University

Assumptions are that the Chicano Movement is male-chauvinistic, and for good reasons. From the start men have dominated it: Cesar Chávez, Reies López Tijerina, Rodolfo Corky Gonzalez, and José Angel Gutiérrez. Many Movement texts stress traditional roles and glorify the male hero with romantic hyperbole. They can be read as male rites of passage which confirm the culture's traditional model of males as dominant and source of action and females as passive and reactive. The binary division of roles differs little from other traditional ethnic groups. I do not claim exclusivity, but rather that this traditional role-definition along sexual lines disparages those who fail to conform and cross those lines of difference, the extreme case being the homosexual.

Homosexuals are absent from the Chicano Movement's self image, and their attempts to gain recognition have had little success. Homophobia may not be more prevalent among Chicanos—though some would aver it— but as products of Mexico and the U.S., neither of which tolerates gays, Chicanos reflect norms of their wider sociocultural context. Yet in homosexuals we ignore and repress a part of our community. Moreover, Chicanismo as a liberation process should consider homosexuals as, ideologically, close fellow travelers.

Surprisingly, the Chicano novel refutes assumptions about Chicano homophobia, for it contains active, albeit limited, discussion about homosexuals and even gay rights. To discover homosexual content and its significance, however, we must foreground homosexuality in texts where emphasis is usually given to ethnic or sociopolitical content. When this is done we discover, first, that of the seven novels published during the first decade of Chicano Movement (1959-1970), five gave central importance to homosexuality. It cannot be said that the Chicano novel ignored homosexuality at the start.

Pocho narrates a father's and son's attempts to realize their ideal of life, despite social codes, U.S. and Mexican, which restrict them. Each frees himself from those expectations and abandons the home to explore new possibilities. While ethnicity is important, so is sexuality, and homosexuality has a dual role: 1) for Juan Rubio, the father, it signifies the extreme opposite of maleness, synonymous with death, yet with some role in human order; 2) it is an alternative mode of being that helps the characters realize themselves in moments of crisis.

For Juan any compromise of macho honor equals emasculation. His is a rigid system of macho behavior: once a man, always a man; therefore, loss of manhood reveals the absence of it from the start. To him a rival amounted to nothing because he was castrated in death, and anyone associated with such a man is also nothing. Homosexuality, thus, is contagious. A man who helped Juan get to California never was allowed the closeness of friendship because Juan suspected him of being gay.

Father and son clash over the former's conception of manliness. In a series of conflicts (Chap. 3, 4, 7, and 10) Juan confronts Richard about the latter's behavior. First, Juan forces Richard to fight a girl (68). Second, Richard must assure Juan that he has had no contact with a homosexual (90). Third, when Juan insists Richard conform to society by marrying and having children, Richard refuses if it means giving up his dreams (131). Finally, on Juan's last night in his home, after a fight in which Juan strikes Richard, the two have a conversation in which Juan recalls the gay to whom he refused friendship (167-169). Richard's comment that homosexuals have a place in society makes Juan accept his son's maturity, which then leads Juan to confess his fear that Richard would turn out gay. This conflictual series culminates in two highly significant acts. First, Juan for the one and only time, expresses love for Richard. Then, before leaving, he kisses his son on the mouth, an action uncharacteristic in Chicano/Mexican culture, only possible because his son has freed him from homophic fear. Thus the topic of machismo/homosexuality is privileged as a catalyst for communication between the male protagonists and for qualitative change in Juan Rubio. Yet, in this context homosexuality is still an opposite pole to manhood. Juan Rubio can express himself, first, because he is sure of his son's heterosexuality, and secondly because he learns tolerance from his son.

The Richard-centered scenes give the topic less traditional connotations. Chapter 4 features a perverse character, Joe Pete Manoel. This Portuguese noble, who tends sheep and ignores the Portuguese community, is a latent homosexual who gets a girl pregnant. When Richard questions life and religion, Joe Pete counsels him to follow his own mind and to use faith until he no longer needs it, then let it go—a perverse philosophy. Yet, from this perverse homosexual Richard learns tolerance. It is Joe Pete's lesson, later voiced by Richard, which opens communication between father and son. Also, Richard has an assimilationist alter-ego figure named Ricky. They are best friends until Richard calls their relationship love (112). Then Ricky suspects Richard of being "queer," which ruins their relationship. This scene also contrasts Richard to his father: whereas Richard cannot be Ricky's real friend because the latter is rigidly heterosexual, Juan refuses friendship to a homosexual. On social and sexual issues, Richard and Juan move in opposite directions, and homosexuality is a key issue.

Ricky's destruction of a relationship through machismo contrasts to the intense friendship offered by a Pachuco leader, Rooster, whom Villarreal describes thus: "His dark hair, Medusa like, curled from his collar in the back almost to his eyebrows." (156) In 1940's context the long hair is charged with feminine connotations, and the adjective adds the destructive, female power from the mythological realm of darkness. This could be simply descriptive, except that Rooster has led Richard into the nether region of violence, fear and death. Later, gays and Pachucos are equated, through the metonymy of "funny people," by the societal spokesman Ricky. And when Richard defends gays because "they take care of each other," (178) he could be talking about Rooster. Richard also equates them by searching out both gays and Pachucos as alternatives to the repression of social and familial norms.

Gays and Pachucos represent lifestyles between societal categories, an intercultural synthesis of binary opposites, perhaps never fully secure and thus always dynamic and exciting. This is consonant with Villarreal's message: Richard rejects choice between one or another in any set of categories, preferring the freedom of dialectical process as more dynamic. Examples abound in the text: night is part of day, evil and good coexist in God; lies are somehow truth; life is most intense in the face of death. Most significant here is that, in the first contemporary Chicano novel, a Chicano hero, the Pachuco, is equated to gays. Villarreal saw that they mirrored one another.

John Rechy's place among Chicano authors has always been disputed. He himself denies having written Chicano novels, concerned as he is primarily with gay literature. Yet Rechy's opus logically extends *Pocho*. *City of Night*'s anonymous Chicano narrator/protagonist leaves home to explore the dark side of U.S. society. Like Juan Rubio, his volatile father, once successful in Mexico, lost social position and self-esteem after immigrating to the U.S. In both novels the son flees repression at home, heading towards areas which frighten but fascinate him: the night, the cold, the wind. Also like Richard, though he fears death, he fears more the nonliving of safe, routine life, and feels most alive when threatened. He too meets an alter-ego who represents stability, but whom he must reject out of fidelity to intense life. He too seeks out those who live alternative modes of existence, some of whom, like Pachucos, flaunt separateness through outlandish dress and speech. Both narratives are epistemological searches for knowledge and desperate religious quests for the sacred—a quest still underlying Rechy's work. The major difference between *Pocho* and Rechy's works is that the latter commences where the former ends, exploring the adult world which Richard is about to enter as *Pocho* closes. And in that world ethnicity ceases to be an explicit subject, becoming one alluded to through the metonymy of the author's background.

While Villarreal attributes utopian virtues to gays—and Pachucos—Rechy withholds privileged status. His gay world darkly parodies the straight one, with gays in search of close approximations of mainstream's goals. Thus Rechy explores the American Dream. His opening paragraph states his parodic intent: "Later I would think of America as one vast City of Night . . . America at night fusing its dark cities into the unmistakable shape of loneliness" (11). In Rechy's work homosexuality is a skewed lense through which readers see their own world from a different angle, thus providing new insights. His message subverts the binary opposition of straight-gay by turning those poles into reflecting mirrors. Utopia on either side is impossible.

By negating the rhetoric of opposites, Rechy shifts to a more essential level: the conflict between form, which imposes static order, and freedom, which manifests itself as fluid chaos, or at least the disorderly lack of conformity. Rechy denies all static order through the negations of monogamy on the sexual plane, secure work on the social, and permanent residency on the geographic. Yet, as I explained elsewhere (Bruce-Novoa, 1979), Rechy the artist cannot avoid form—his texts are carefully structured. The conflict pits Apollonina against Dionysian impulses, and Rechy responds like Nietzsche in *The Birth of Tragedy*: tragedy in its constant mixture and subversion of set form which avoids the stasis of final resolution by maintaining an ongoing dialectical process of the intermingling of opposites: Life on the border.[1] Life as fluid process, but also as the tragic loneliness of outlaws, those who refuse to embrace one or the other pole of traditional difference. Both Villarreal's Richard and Rechy (through a long series of his characters) prefer to locate themselves between absolutes to live more authentically.

Floyd Salas' *Tattoo the Wicked Cross* (1967) preserves the negativity traditionally associated with homosexuality. A boy tries to preserve his integrity and self-esteem in prison, where his enemy threatens to subjugate him through homosexual rape. When he is raped, he adopts the criminal code by murdering his assailant. The homosexual act signifies ultimate destruction in terms of normal society. In Salas' traditional, strictly binary code, everything is either fish or fowl. The gang rape is not simply violence, but a "making queens out of 'em forever" (37), only countervailed by murder. Salas also compared his protagonist to a Pachuco, but it is unclear whether his protagonist fails to meet Pachuco standards, or becomes like a Pachuco when rape makes him a social pariah. The latter reading would repeat Villarreal's metonymic equation of the two groups. Which ever way, clearly Salas used both terms negatively.

In his semiautobiographical works *The Autobiography of a Brown Buffalo* (1972) and *The Revolt of Cockroach the People* (1973), Oscar Zeta Acosta does not idealize gays from a distance like Villarreal, nor feature them like Rechy, but his references to gays become leitmotif of negative signification. Acosta's books could be satiric parodies of Villareal's and Rechy's. Acosta too voyages cross country in search of himself, discovering, like Rechy, societal hypocrisy. His trip takes him through rites of passage until he discovers his affinity for social deviants. Also like Rechy, his view of his chosen people—Chicanos in his case—debunks utopian ideals. Horts Tonn has accurately commented that Acosta portrayed Chicanos as a multifaceted, highly fragmented group, some of whom are involved in a Movement devoid of ideology or strategy, and who are open to racial, cultural or sexual pluralism. In the end, like Rechy's characters, Acosta withdraws to his private space to maintain his integrity through the written word. Finally, Acosta also mixes Dionysian content with carefully structured Apollonian form.

Yet, despite Acosta's claim to defend the rights of all cockroaches—meaning all the downtrodden—homosexuals are excluded and branded as the enemy.[2] At the start Acosta depicts himself as a liberal, sexually tolerant lawyer, yet "faggot" becomes his supreme insult. At first it is lightly *despectivo*, meaning old or boring, but by the end of *Brown Buffalo* Acosta groups homosexuals with society's dregs, using guilt by association: "winos and fags" (197). The negative synonymy is even more pronounced in *Cockroach*, where homosexual and enemy result synonyms. The ultimate effect recalls that in Salas, homosexuality signifies the evil other, the inhuman, the trace of condemnation. Despite Acosta's obvious satiric intent in every facet of his texts, the homophobia is still offensive.

After Acosta's satires, almost a decade passed before another Chicano novel would feature homosexuality: Sheila Ortiz Taylor's *Faultine* (1982), a lesbian novel. It and *Spring Forward/Fall Back* (1985) are utopian novels which posit the alternative of loving, harmonious, humane, repressionless extended families centered around lesbians. Like *Pocho* and Rechy's works, *Faultine*, through its central image, focuses on living intensely in an in-between zone of constant shifting and flux, thus turning a negative term positive through rhetorical manipulation. And so many characters with different sexual preferences appear that the lesbian couple's eventual victory mirrors that of many others. In other words Ortiz Taylor equates the lesbian struggle to that of feminists, gay men, straight couples, the aged, prostitutes, and, by extension, all people restricted by social norms or traditional role definitions. It proposes the alternative of creating one's own life, and in utopian fashion everything works out. The text itself flaunts its improbability, but convinces through the power of desire. When the protagonist accepts her lesbianism, the texts has prepared us to applaud the decision as correct, honest and liberating. When it culminates in the double marriage of a male homosexual couple and the lesbian lovers, the texts has taught us to approve and agree that this is the best ending possible. Ortiz Taylor heaps so many positive connotations on this lesbian couple's lifestyle that lesbianism becomes synonymous with liberation.

Spring Forward/Fall Back is less engrossing, probably because it shifts to introspective realism. Yet, despite admitting that lesbians too have problematic relationships, the novel affirms the need for spaces in which people can pursue alternative modes of existence. The right to preserve old neighborhoods against developers, or a house which sheltered an extended lesbian family, mirror any group's attempt to maintain its space within and against the dominant society. That the novel ends with the protagonist vowing to write about the ideal lesbian family, which she calls the frontier family, is similar to the need to write Chicano novels where culture can survive, and from which the group can draw inspiration. That she calls it a frontier family once again alludes to the need to live on the edge between social absolutes, but also emphasizes the desire to place distance between oneself and the dominant society. It is the difference between emphasizing the edge as a border or frontier. This second novel is less optimistic and more realistic in that the lesbian utopia is seen as threatened and in need of rescue. But that, also, would compare to Chicano texts which see our culture in a similar light. Ortiz Taylor's production is worthy of our attention and support, even though many will complain that she does not focus on truly Chicano issues. Actually, much like Rechy, but in more optimistic tone, she shows us that Chicanos can be leading figures in other literary movements.

Our last work for discussion is Arturo Islas' *The Rain God*. The narrator recreates his family through writing. He creates multiple perspectives, orders them and chooses the content. In other words, we do not have a family history from varied points of view, but the familial context through which one character, the narrator, depicts himself. This difference is essential to understanding the significance of homosexuality.

Although the family is said to center around the grandmother, Mama Chona, the narration displaces that focus onto his gay Uncle Felix. Joyful and friendly, Felix was the favorite nephew of a black sheep great aunt. These less than respectable relatives embody vitality and passion, while the rest are repressed, alienated, psychologically disturbed. "When Felix was a child he would . . . dance when the storm clouds passed over . . . Neither Mama Chona, nor later his own family, could stop him. 'You'll be struck by lightning,' they said. 'Good. I'll die dancing.' " (114) Felix celebrates life even to the point of death, and the chapter dedicated to him is called "Rain Dancer." At the death of Mama Chona, when Felix's spirit comes to his dying mother, the narrator remarks that he—Miguel Chico—"Felt the Rain God come into the room." (179) Uncle Felix is linked to the title through its attribution to him directly and indirectly in the text.

Miguel Chico and Felix are bound metonymically through action and the character involved in the action performed. However, by the end of the novel the narrator has liberated himself from the death grasp of Mama Chona, by substituting his Uncle Felix for himself, and by displacing the source of power and action from the grandmother to the uncle. Miguel Chico is a narrator of tales, a reteller as he is called, who takes liberties with his material, "arranging various facts, adding others, reordering . . . putting himself in . . . removing himself" to create versions that "were happier than their 'real' counterparts." (26) He writes his story to restructure the family and life around the homosexual uncle and to create himself as Felix's heir. The text justifies his marginated familial status by appropriating a central role in the unseen family tradition. He continues the line of those who enjoyed life, preferred passion to repression, and who had to live their passions in secret, hidden from the repressive center of familiar authority. The narrator/protagonist Miguel Chico lives at a distance, hidden from the eyes of the family. His life is never explored like that of others because he prefers indirect revelation, not simply as a member of the family, but, more importantly, as the novelist, the creator of the text. Although his activities must be kept secret, like Uncle Felix's, they are the real center of family life.

Islas' narrator is less forthcoming than Ortiz Taylor's. While the latter's protagonists come out of the closet, Islas' invites us in. Yet both treat the subject from a new perspective. Rechy's images from within the gay world spring from the view point of an outlaw among outlaws, the gay hustler. These new authors locate their characters and narrators in a more centralized position within their group.

This brief survey of homosexuality in the Chicano novel reveals no consistent view, but does show that it has been treated in some dozen texts and from multiple perspectives. All in all the topic of homosexuality, like that of ethnicity, produces different reactions, and is used, or abused, in varied manners. What is heartening is that in the majority of cases, homosexuals and homosexual acts are not subjected to stereotypical prejudice. If the novel gives us an accurate reading of the Chicano community—a question in itself debatable—we can say that our community is less sexually repressive than we might expect. If nothing else, among Chicano novelists there are varying attitudes and a willingness to address the topic. This makes the Chicano novel a progressive space of dialogue, an appropriate space in and through which a more androgenous and humane Chicano identity may be forged.

[1]"Should our analysis have established the point that the Apollonian element in tragedy has by means of its illusion gained a complete victory over the Dionysian . . . at the most essential point this Apollonian illusion is dissolved and annihilated . . . this drama attains as a whole an effect of tragedy, the Dionysian once again dominates. Tragedy closes with a sound which could never emanate from the realm of Apollonian art. And the Apollonian illusion thereby reveals itself as what it really is—the assiduous veiling during the performance of the tragedy of the intrinsically Dionysian wisdom, and even denies itself and its Apollonian conspicuousness. So that the intricate relation of the Apollonian and the Dionysian in tragedy may really be symbolized by a fraternal union of the two deities: Dionysus speaks the language of Apollo; Apollo, however, finally speaks the language of Dionysus; and so the highest goal of tragedy and of art in general is attained." Nietzsche, 1071.

[2]I am grateful to Steven K. Baird, a Yale student, who shared his insights as a homosexual into Acosta's treatment of his group.

Acosta, Oscar Zeta. *The Autobiography of a Brown Buffalo*. San Francisco: Straight Arrow Books, 1972.
———. *The Revolt of the Cockroach People*. San Francisco: Straight Arrow Books, 1973.
Baird, Steven K. "Accosting Acosta, From One Cockroach to Another." Unpublished essay, Yale University, 1982.
Bruce-Novoa. "In Search of the Honest Outlaw: John Rechy." *Minority Voices*, 3/1 (Fall 1979) pp. 37–45.
Islas, Arturo. *The Rain God*. Palo Alto: Alexandrian Press, 1984.
Nietzsche. *The Birth of Tragedy*. In *The Philosophy of Nietzsche*. New York: The Modern Library, 1954.

Ortiz Taylor, Sheila. *Faultline*. Tallahassee: Naiad Press, 1982.
____*Spring Forward/Fall Back*. Tallahassee: Naiad Press, 1985.
Rechy, John. *City of Night*. New York: Grove Press, 1963.
____*This Day's Death*. New York: Grove Press, 1969.
Salas, Floyd. *Tattoo the Wicked Cross*. New York: Grove Press, 1967.
Tonn, Horst. Untersuchungen zum englischigen Chicano-Roman: Ernest Garza, *Barrio Bay*; Oscar Zeta Acosta, *The Revolt of the Cockroach People*; Rudolfo A. Anaya, *Bless Me, Ultima*. Dissertation Freien Universitat Berlin, 1986.
Villareal, José Antonio. *Pocho*. Garden City: Doubleday, 1959.

Internal Exile in the Chicano Novel: Structure and Paradigms

Francisco A. Lomelí
University of California-Santa Barbara

Much of Chicano literature has portrayed culture as a dynamic process of conflict between the evils of assimilation and the means of resistance. The struggle is conceptualized as one in which inequities are intimated, described and denounced. What emerges—although at times subtly and other times overtly—is a strong sense of not appropriately belonging within a society that sets unqualified conditions to their inclusion. Therefore, when Rodolfo "Corky" Gonzales wrote in *I Am Joaquin* (1976) "My fathers/ have lost the economic battle and won/ the struggle of cultural survival,"[1] these words hit a tender chord in Chicano historical sensibility and articulated, perhaps for the first time, their irresolvable conflict which characterizes Chicano literature. Some writers have felt compelled, even obsessed, or simply propelled to carry forth that line of reasoning and consciousness. Part of the motivating force deals with overcoming the general perception that Chicanos do not form an integral component of American society because of their frequent label as outsiders, recent immigrants or "not typical Americans."

Even the most superficial perusal of the history of the United States demonstrates the common plight of immigrant groups in this regard: retaining an ethnic identity yet somehow belonging to American society. Given that options such as absorption into mainstream society or adoption of makeshift values are limited and not always attractive, Chicano writers seek unique geo-poetic representations of the relationship with their social milieu. This study will examine the issue of internal exile in three novels, each possessing a distinct twist on how the author sees and reacts to the experience of exile. The works with which to expand this concept are as follows: *Victuum* (1976) by Isabella Ríos, *Pelón Drops Out* (1979) by Celso A. de Casas, and *Puppet* (1985) by Margarita Cota-Cárdenas.

The theme of internal exile is not only a literary phenomenon. The lack of general acceptance, or minimal acceptability, of Chicano literature within the current body of American literary circles reflects how Chicanos are viewed in their society. Their social marginality transfers over so as to consider them less-than-authentic American writers. Consequently, many

Chicano writers feel compelled to choose an independent and autonomous—some would emphasize unattached—posture toward the act of creating literature. In other words, the concern of identity emerges as a central question: being part of a larger congregation or becoming an entity unto oneself. Each author resolves the issue in a personal fashion that corresponds with the intent of the novel. For example, José A. Villarreal in *Pocho* (1959) grapples with the idea of being a new and different type of "American" of Mexican descent by accentuating his individuality and resisting all labels that infringe on his quest for personal identity. In *City of Night* (1963), by John Rechy, the protagonist operates within the confines of a reduced group of individuals whose homosexuality is represented as illegitimate from the perspective of an intolerant society. Tomás Rivera, in . . . *y no se lo tragó la tierra* (1971), allows to unfold an internal exile that oscillates between madness and affirmation while creating a renewed sense of existential purpose. Miguel Méndez' *Peregrinos de Aztlán* (1974) depicts uprooted characters in a pilgrimage searching for a place (Aztlán) to which they *can* belong; the degree to which they are exploited determines their social worth. In another example, Ron Arias, in *The Road to Tamazunchale* (1975), presents a dying old man whose only possibility of successfully defying death is through the imagination and dreams; he becomes an exile of life—literally and figuratively. Finally, Alejandro Morales, in *Caras viejas y vino nuevo* (1975), proposes a route of escape from a denigrating and decadent barrio by learning to decipher the elements of oppression and the limits of real or imagined walls.

The Chicano novel constantly emphasizes inner and outer space, the individual's place in society, and problems related to ethnicity and culture. Exile, then, is rarely horizontal, but rather vertical, oftentimes represented as a form of existential ascent into the self. In some cases, the condition is prefigured by the simple option to utilize Spanish as the mode of communication; thus, language in itself encompasses the prism through which a world view of culture is filtered. This language choice favoring Spanish can be understood as a form of self-exile and defiance within a country so intolerant toward other languages. Some Chicano writers consciously follow this trend because of the relevance they see in developing works from their own cultural slant. A sense of nonconformity is transformed into authentic registers of expression that highlight Chicano qualities.

The theme of exile is indeed one of the most perplexing topics of the twentieth century. By general definition, it implies geographical movement or ostracism from one country to another for socio-political, religious or economic reasons. However, exile can be expanded to take on psychological and moral values. Literature of exile tempers much of this perspective, although a clear distinction is posited by Rafael Conte in *Narraciones de la España desterrada* (1970) when he states: "La literatura del exilio será . . . un fenómeno individual, nunca colectivo, aunque sí masivo."[2] Another author, Heinrich Mann, in *Exile Literature, 1933–1945* (1968), observes that "Emigration . . . is the voice of a people which has grown silent."[3] With the advent of numerous situations dictating the need to mobilize from one area to another, exile literature has consequently become a more commonplace phenomenon in this century. As John M. Spalek and Robert F. Bell have noted in *Exile: The Writer's Experience*, "Much of twentieth-century literature, especially from the European continent has been written in exile."[4] It has also acquired new modes of expression, giving depth to the whole notion of exile.

Paul Ilie is one of the principal figures to expand the general notion of exile by distinguishing between internal exile and that which is a mere change in physical space. His conceptualizations in *Literatura y exilio interior* (1980) apply well to the Chicano writers' state of mind and the psycho-moral sense of alienation.[5] The European and Chicano experiences quickly diverge at this point: whereas the former tends to be guided by what Paul Tabori terms a type of *puer aeternus*, a perpetual adolescence or virus of longing for the homeland,[6] the latter suffers a process of disenchantment with the infatuating elements of North American materialism. Clearly, the motives and conceptualization of internal exile are quite distinct.

If on the one hand Chicanos nostalgically try to salvage images and customs of Mexican culture in a North American environment, they soon discover that their isolation is not self-imposed, but greatly enhanced by a society that essentially, and tragically, rejects them. Long-term residency (in some cases seven or eight generations found in New Mexico and southern Colorado) is often still not sufficient to be acknowledged as full-fledged American by Anglo society. More recent immigrants come to realize that their ethnic background becomes a cross to bear for as long as they wish to carry it. The passageway is usually one of cultural co-optation as the ultimate alternative in order to facilitate total assimilation. Until they "cross over," the most viable integration is at best a relative or marginal one, enabling them to pass through the filtering process of social acceptability. Chicanos have reacted and responded to this Catch-22 predicament by partially separating themselves with the intent of participating only on their own terms. This consciousness assumes a distinct expression of some form of rebellion because Chicanos recognize that the only real option is total surrender of all that one is and would like to become.

Many paradigms exist to describe the Chicano experience of dealing with the problems related to integration and rejection. The political model of an "internal colony", as proposed by Rodolfo Acuña in *Occupied America: The Chicano's Struggle Toward Liberation* (1972),[7] is perhaps one of the most appropriate with which to begin to define the dialectical relationship between Chicanos and Anglo society. The hyphenated identity and labels related to Mexican-Americans still remain as a central issue to comprehending their role and place within the United States. Although the "internal colony" model might be regarded as unjustifiable in purely economic terms, the symbolic intent of that model applies in diffused cultural terms due to encirclement factors. Chicano culture exists, participates and evolves by juggling elements of two cultures, while recognizing that the more Mexican side is subjected to greater pressures of enduring. Other paradigms of total assimilation or complete resistance to partially assimilating are becoming obsolete. Chicanos seem to adapt but in their town terms. Therefore, exile in the Chicano sense should not be confused with being a refugee as if getting away from something. An exile suggests seeking something and in the Chicano situation it is imperative to keep in mind that the American Southwest is still generally regarded by the Mexican populace as a place that was Mexico. Emigration, then, is viewed more within the confines of migration, since the geographical displacement is neither drastic nor unfamiliar. Realization of internal exile occurs when the Mexican or Chicano is made to feel as a "foreigner in his native land," as David J. Weber mentions.[8]

In an important study, *Exiles at Home: A Story of Literature in Nineteenth Century America*, Daniel Marder claims that isolation and alienation are the greatest contributors to such a state: "The isolated individual is outside of society while the alienated is hostile as well as outside."[9] Internal exile marks a process of seeking a center, or one's own space, while existing in the periphery. This paradox corresponds well to the dilemma depicted in the Chicano novel. Particularly acute is the admission of not belonging to any *one* country, linguistically, psychologically and ideologically. A cultural dislodgement emerges, thus forcing the person to find refuge from within from which a world view is subsequently structured. As a result, a highly subjective and experiential perspective becomes the vantage point, or, according to Luis Farré, "Aislarse equivale a trascender para valorizar y juzgar."[10] Furthermore, exile and existentialism are not synonymous because the experience of exile could be considered symptomatic of the existential mode of perception.[11] Most notably, exile deals more with a spiritual posture or point of view than a state based on material means. The exile of which we speak encompasses an internal dialogue, a way of integrating what the person regards as significant. Exile provides a mechanism or system of values in order to cope with an external world.

In the Chicano novel, both a sense of separation and turbulence pervades, but usually for very different reasons. In assessing the genre as a whole, it becomes evident that Chicano writers view their relationship with society as one filled with apprehension and void of trust. A strong sense of distance between the individual and the milieu predominates and writers respond with their own fictional creations to exercise free-will. For example, in *Victuum* (1976) by Isabella Ríos, the protagonist, Valentina Ballesternos, sees her life as quite apart from others. In the form of a *Bildungsroman*, the work traces a woman's life story from the fetal stage to a mature and aging woman. A female sense of the world emanates throughout the narrative and the text functions as if it *were* the person: all action is filtered through the eyes and ears of the main character. Discourse is entirely subjective as a direct reflection of her psyche. A witness of every detail, the first-person narrator appropriately defines all experience from her perspective. The life-long trajectory extends from a pre-conscious level to a supra-conscious state, consisting of an inner space that is prescribed by psychic phenomena. A persistent emphasis on an internal posture has the protagonist looking out from within, suggesting that she receives stimuli for which she was preconditioned. In this sense the narrator becomes the creator of her own order and of everything that the reader experiences in the text.

Victuum operates as a personally encoded work. On the one hand, folkloric tradition dictates that an onion skin-like membrane at birth will endow her with a highly developed sixth sense or innate powers to experience meta-reality. But, her psychic abilities will also allow her to transcend the physical world through visions and dreams of both future and past. Space and time for her only exist as integral parts of her introspection. In the opening scene, the self-description as a fetus meditating on the philosophical note of "sound am I"[12] denotes a strong tendency to associate herself with a fourth-dimension, captured only through intuition. She does not identify with any one specific social group because her ultimate motive, a quest for knowledge, is not sanctioned by society. On the contrary, she has suffered persecution and doubts—even about her sanity. Inherited from her mother, her powers provide her with a sense of female continuity and a secret she must keep to herself. This supernatural connection with her mother establishes a conflict with her society which ostracizes Valentina. Dispelling stigmas and innuendoes, she succumbs to intuition and indulges in a series of extra-sensory experiences through visions and dreams, and coming in contact with a number of historical, mythological, fictitious and fantastic figures. If earlier limited by boundaries and demarcations, at the end she totally defies them through a near magical journey into the realm of thought and ideas that manifest themselves in a metaphysical state. Her final encounter with Victuum, an extraterrestrial being, marks a mystical step into a universe of ideas, thus culminating in infinity and true liberation. To Valentina, ultimate reality is experience gained through intuition in order to connect with meta-reality. Only then is she able to supersede the limitations set by a physical world. Although trapped by the mundane, her real motivation consists in acquiring enlightenment and knowledge about other horizons. Her internal exile is further augmented by having to keep her visions a secret, so her option is to live a double life. Subjected to social circumventions, Valentina seeks out the liberating effects of imagination and knowledge with which to formulate a new world view. By creating her own time, space and personages, she displays an affinity for renovating her social order in order to become an integral part of it. In a real sense, she constructs her own world to replace the one in which she lives.

In a second work, *Pelón Drops Out*[13] (1979) by Celso A. de Casas, the process of separation and exile is humorously treated in a tongue-in-cheek parody of *The Teachings of Don Juan* by Carlos Castañeda. The protagonist, Pelón Palomares, whose first name literally means "baldheaded," embodies someone lacking street-smartness or common sense. The down-and-out qualities in his character suggest that he is out of tune with his surroundings. Thus, it comes naturally to him to drop-out from society. Not quite synchronized with his milieu, he withdraws and seeks out an apprenticeship into the world of "working warriors," actually cement masonry. His two mentors, Gerónimo Vidrios and Santos Trig(u)eño, lead Pelón in a rite of passage designed to release him from "the spell of the cesos (sic) de caca" (p. 28). The magical journey into another dimension offers him the opportunity to overcome institutional conditioning and thus satisfy a spiritual inquiry into the self. Although his means are quite distinct, he parallels what Valentina in *Victuum* upheld as primordial: the acquisition of power through knowledge. Described as suffering from the curse of the *tapado*, or stuffed with useless matter, he knows his recourse is to break away from learned molds and bid a fundamental transformation at the hands of his philosophical but cynical mentors.

The internal structure of the novel is dictated by an ardent search to find a place where Pelón might achieve self-actualization through either dreams or visions. A form of utopia where the identity is fully reconciled, it consists of a " . . . fifth world where reality (is) beyond dimensions, above time, wider than infinity of heavens" (p. 29). Significantly, this trip must maintain a cult or secretive quality in order to achieve the desired results. Partly fueled by gut-humor and visceral descriptions, the protagonist dedicates most of his time to following instructions on how to reach a pure spiritual state. The ascending stages of purification are induced by the use of magical substances, such as concoctions called *chilepuro*, sacred *verdolagas*, *tolondrones pa' los preguntones*, and magic *mocos*. Obviously a slapstick comedy a la Cheech and Chong, and a spoof on cult drugs, Pelón's serious search seems camouflaged by these giddy underpinnings and frivolous methods. This is only a smoke-screen to the profound expression of isolation. The magical trips become metaphorical representations of his response to his internal exile, while at the same time a search for another level of reality. The protagonist's challenge to overcome fear in the form of the *cu-cui*, or the bogeyman, is analogous to the more serious and sublime methodolody in *The Teachings of Don Juan*. As one of his mentors states, "Fear is nothing more than memory." (p. 99) Therefore, it is imperative he come to understand his Indian part, his Chicano consciousness and his freedom from ignorance. To accomplish his end, he desires contact with a magical land through a fantasy dream. As one Indian told Pelón, "We only know that this land is a place where we can be ourselves, where we can live on our terms, and survive on the basis of our ability to deal with the land" (p. 108). The central idea, although decorated with humor and madness, clearly points to locating such a place, that is, another realm of existence where the individual may become more complete.

Pelón Drops Out appeals to other forms of logic and perspective. This allows for the theme to be more palatable to the reader without having to account for ideological overtones. Nonetheless, one of the repeated ideas is to escape prison by entering the imagination. Pelón's sense of dropping out, therefore, is a reminder to seek more authentic forms beyond societal conditioning. The model of mystical salvation quickly gives way to a politically and socially motivated concern.

The novel's humor might be taken as mockery of the search-for-identity theme so commonly found in Chicano literature, but the joke should rest on the medium, not the message. The insistent play-on-words functions as a cathartic instrument; however, the search for a place like Aztlán is indeed a serious proposal. Dropping out in this case implies a rejection of the social milieu that standardizes people into ridding them of their atavistic origins. The novel, then, satirizes cultural innocence of the sort that does not establish Chicano reality as its true basis. In sum, Pelón opts toward a self-contained perception of the world underscored by language and naturalist symbols (i.e. a sense of place) in order to make contact with his origins. By implication, Chicanos need to remove their cultural blinders to see things as they are or as they wish them to be.

In a very recent novel, *Puppet*[14] by Margarita Cota-Cárdenas, the protagonist Petra Leyva unfolds a most fascinating process: she writes a novel—the one we read—which represents her burgeoning from a previous state of inaction, passivity and internal exile. She has in a sense been separated from her true self or alienated from what she is capable of being. In the novel she becomes an instrument to protest the tragic and suspicious death of a young pachucho named Tony López, commonly known as Puppet. The leitmotif "¿No lo vites en las news?", while referring to the media coverage of that death, turns into a constant ring in the protagonist's conscience. No longer able to continue her self-deception and fatalistic fear, she now feels compelled to act on Puppet's behalf. Thus, she assumes the role of a double spokesperson: she speaks for Tony López and herself, both representing an analogous form of death. With a newly acquired sense of purpose and awareness, she is better equipped to conquer her illusions and fairy tales. It is both significant and ironic that Petra Leyva begins to live thanks to Puppet's death. In other words, she initiates a noticeable withdrawal from her internal exile and abnegation at the same time that Puppet enters Nirvana. A symbiotic relationship exists between the two as they go in opposite directions.

The novel represents the story of how a harsh social reality imposes itself on a woman accustomed to indulge in romantic divagations and daydreams. The crudeness of violence against the pachuco youth forces the protagonist to break out of her shell of mental and social paralysis. Puppet's death at the hands of police stirs in her a series of doubts and leads her to consider arbitrary and/or racial violence. More importantly, Puppet's name suggests manipulation on both a social and personal level.

Furthermore, this may be understood as a sharp reminder to certain marginalized youth of the drastic measures society may take to rid itself of undesirables. But, Petra interprets his death differently: she gains inner strength and direction in her otherwise useless life by vindicating the young man and denouncing the tragedy as a socially premeditated act. The constant ringing of the telephone throughout the novel, while breaking the narrative in abrupt fashion, operates as a Brechtian element to rattle the reader's suspension of disbelief. The telephone becomes one more motif on how and why the protagonist needs to break away from her internal exile, a state comprised of solitude, alienation and inertia. Although this may seem as a self-inflicted condition, we discover that it is also attributed to a society's relegation of her—something which before she had not realized. The telephone, as a symbol of communication, here becomes a repeated attempt to make contact with other people. Thus, Petra is better prepared to look outside of herself as part of a network for change. The externalization from her own encirclement now figures as a force to reckon with, principally due to her renewed vigor of purpose. Petra's prolonged internal exile, then, teaches her a vital lesson of resorting to her inner strength in order to refocus her attitude on life. By overcoming her own personal absurdity and impotence, she soon discovers the redeeming quality of acquiring a social commitment on someone else's behalf.

The novel operates much in the manner of a closed circuit constantly being interrupted. The language, as the line of communication, is an attempt to break a long-held silence on the part of the protagonist. It represents a breaking out of doldrums and a slap on the face for those whose conscience is dormant. In that context, the final scene reveals an act of communion between at least three persons (Petra, her husband and Puppet), a trinity of renewed solidarity to vindicate the young man's death. Their voices, joined as three telephone party lines, form a collective chorus that challenges the reader with the final assertion: "¿qué esperas?" Petra manages effectively to shed her previous defeatism by overcoming her demoralized state. The ultimate lesson for her is that the individual needs to act upon society in order to shape it into the image of oneself or of those who are deemed voiceless.

These examples illustrate how Chicano writers offer diverse and innovative approaches to the concept of internal exile. In *Victuum, Pelón Drops Out* and *Puppet*, a particularly keen awareness of such a condition permeates the narrative. A separation from society is clearly in evidence, even if the causes are not always examined or laid out. As metaphors of a world view, each offers a self-contained message with certain constants of not belonging to the social order described. An insular perspective usually emerges to delineate the person's reclusion, oftentimes within his/her own mind frame. As a general rule, the protagonists do not advocate an utopian point of view per se, although they hint at finding a sanctuary of free thinking and self-actualization. In each case, they experience a drift or estrangement with their respective environment, forcing them to fabricate or imagine an alternative existence which opposes their own. Their story, as a paradigm of the free spirit, only represents the anecdotal form of their intuition to exercise creativity and authentication. For instance, in *Victuum* Valentina defies space and time by substituting them with another universal order that consists of a continuum of ideas, knowledge and infinity. In spite of his charades, Pelón in *Pelón Drops Out* aspires to coming in contact with a place where he might become what he thinks he is. Petra, in *Puppet*, is successful in regaining part of her lost conscience, thus overpowering her own dehumanization as well as that of the young victim. The three novels underscore the importance of imagination to overcome internal exile. A psycho-moral view of the individual's role in society is consequently purported, not as a mystical union with a divine being, but rather, as a purging effect to reach a higher order of realization. Since the protagonists do not necessarily *belong* or *fit* in their immediate locus, they fantasize and invent their own space while ridding themselves of the "foreigners in their native land" stigma. They become creators and inhabitants of their inventions. In conclusion, each text, as a fictitious artifice, offers a double commentary: first, on the entrapments of internal exile as a social experience; and, second on the predicaments involved with formulating the groundwork for a new nation. This could very well be Aztlán.

[1] Rodolfo "Corky" Gonzalez, *I am Joaquín* (New York: Bantam Books, 1972), p. 6. The original copyright was in 1967 by the author and the Crusade for Justice in Denver, Colorado.

[2] Rafael Conte, *Narraciones de la España desterrada* (Barcelona: EDHASA, 1970), p. 14.

[3] See *Exile Literature, 1933-1945* (Bad Godesberg: Inter Nations, 1968), p. 18.

[4] See the cited work from the University of North Carolina Press at Chapel Hill, North Carolina, 1982, p. xi. They also add that some of the highest quality literature has been produced by writers found in that condition, such as Thomas Mann, Nelly Sachs, Ramón Sender, Alexander Solzhenitsyn, Rafael Alberti, Witold Gombrowicz, Czeslaw Milosz, Vladimir Nabokov, and E. M. Cioran. To this list many Latin Americans, among some of the most noteworthy, could be added, such as Mario Benedetti, Julio Cortázar, Ramón Amaya Amador, and others.

[5] Although this author approaches our concept of internal exile, it should be noted that his primary concern is to examine the various forms of exile evident in Spain under the Franco regime between 1939 and 1975. One of the principal differences with his positions and precepts involves a relative legitimacy on the part of Spaniards and others to recognize an "exile" literature related to the Spanish experience. His observations appear more obvious because of the recognized "two Spanish literatures," perhaps also termed official and unofficial.

[6] For further discussion on these pertinent points, see Paul Tabori's *The Anatomy of Exile: A Semantic and Historical Study* (London: George P. Harrap, 1972), pp. 32-56.

[7] As an historian he advances a number of arguments for his thesis based in part on original interpretations and Third World politics. The book was published in San Francisco by Canfield Press in 1972. Another useful work that supports

Acuña's central idea is Carey McWilliams' seminal study, *North From Mexico: The Spanish-Speaking People of the United States* (Lippincott: n.p., 1949).

[8]The idea forms the central thesis of David J. Weber's *Foreigners in Their Native Land* (Albuquerque: The University of New Mexico Press, 1973).

[9]Daniel Marder, *Exiles at Home: A Story of Literature in Nineteenth Century America* (New York: University Press of America, 1984), p. 6.

[10]See Luis Farré's *Aislamiento y comunicación: enfoques psicológico, filosófico y teolgico* (Buenos Aires: Editorial y Libreria La Aurora, S.R.L., 1970), p. 5.

[11]John M. Spalek and Robert F. Bell, editors, *Exile: The Writer's Experience* (Chapel Hill, North Carolina: University of North Carolina Press, 1982), pp. 87.

[12]Isabella Ríos, *Victuum* (Ventura, California: Diana-Etna, Inc., 1976), p. 1. It is worth noting that the work was copyrighted in 1975 which competes with Berta Ornelas' *Come Down From the Mound* as the first novel by a Chicana writer after the literary renaissance of 1965.

[13]It was originally published by Tonatiuh International at Berkeley, California, in 1979. All pagination comes from this edition.

[14]Published by Relámpago Books Press (Austin, Texas) in 1985.

Chicano and Nuyorican Literature—
Elements of a Democratic and Socialist Culture in the U.S. of A.?

Dieter Herms
University of Bremen

I. Introduction

The somewhat schematic-sounding title terminology goes back to V. I. Lenin's theory of the two cultures, formulated in his 1913 essay "Critical Remarks on the National Question,"[1] where he stated that in "each national culture," there are by necessity "elements of a democratic and socialist culture," of a "second culture" versus the "ruling" culture of the "first." The proposition generally put forward in this paper is that, however historically limited, Lenin's observation might still help us for a sharper understanding of progressive ethnic literature; and, more specifically: examples from Puerto Rican and Chicano literature in the U.S. are here looked at, not only in their "national," but also in their "international" dimension, contributing to an overall "second culture" of the U.S.A.

My first attempt (internationally) to look at just Chicano literature in terms of the framework of the Lenin formula,[2] was partially rejected, partially modified by Lauro Flores.[3] In order to translate the original concept into the multi-ethnic, multicultural situation of the modern United States, a more careful definition of "nation" as a historical category would be necessary, he argues, for: "Tal actitud llevada al extremo se destila con grotesca exactitud en la expresión racista: 'they are all the same' ('todos son iguales')."[4]

Flores is right in emphasizing that Lenin referred to the dialectic of two cultures *within* smaller national identities, such as the Ukrainian or Georgian. Lenin, however, also observed that the majority of Ukrainian workers is under the impact of the Great-Russian culture, a historical condition which is structurally comparable to the more modern situation of Mexican Americans, Native Americans, Black Americans and Puerto Ricans in the U.S.

Flores does not pay attention to Lenin's notion of an "international democratic culture and the workers' movement in the whole world," which stresses in "*each* national culture *only* its democratic and socialist elements as 'counterweight" ' to the overall and powerful bourgeois and reactionary culture. By arguing in terms of almost the big historical "blocks" nationally and internationally, Lenin might well be foreshadowing Gramsci.

The approach, then, favored here, is looking independently at the uninterchangeable specific Chicano, American Indian, Afro-American, and Nuyorican quality of the respective histories, politics, aesthetics, cultures, and literatures, but at the same time examining the cross-cultural, anti-imperialist, democratic and socialist quality, thus identifying elements of an ideology common to them all. Historically speaking, we are viewing the U.S. as a multicultural, multi-ethnic "nation;" but within the "coloso del norte," the "belly of the monster," we observe smaller tribes or nations, their differences and their similarities.

I shall first look at four literary examples, then summarize the potential relevance of the Lenin theory for a modern context, and in conclusion, relate these findings to the overall oeuvre of the four authors.

II. Four Texts

Piri Thomas' *Down These Mean Streets*, today sometimes looked down upon as an "ethnic autobiography," which only perpetuates the "culture of poverty,"[5] is still the most widely read Nuyorican piece of literature. The prologue, in angry rhythmic prose, reveals the author's ambivalence about the city of New York, and Harlem in particular:

> This is a bright *mundo*, my streets, my *barrio de noche*,
> With its thousands of lights, hundreds of millions of colors,
> Mingling with noises, swinging street sounds of cars and curses,
> Sounds, of joys and sobs that make music. . . [6]

His speech is characterized by parallelisms and contrasts, the alliteration of cars and curses, the dichotomy, joys and sobs, love and hate. The juxtaposition of isolation and warmth is captured best by the image of the "great big dirty Christmas tree with lights, but no fucking presents." The concluding note is one of unmitigated hatred, of anger and selfishness as the only possible mode of survival: "And I begin to listen to the sounds inside me. Get angry, get hating angry, and you won't be scared . . . "[7]

This, then, is the overture to an autobiographical novel about adolescence and the experience of racism, about a Puerto Rican's quest for blackness, about the search for identity, not primarily of a Puerto Rican in

New York, but rather of an American black. It is the internalized racism, the transferred racism operating within the black consciousness, which generates the quest, not only the intrafamilial racism of his brother, but specifically that of the black guy in the subway, who says: "Will you look at that damn nigger with that white girl?"[8]

Thus, Piri's quest for the black roots, the trip with his friend Brew into the Jim Crow deep old slave South provides the setting in which his struggle takes place, the struggle to free himself from the attitude of superiority which Puerto Ricans of Spanish descendant have over Afro-Americans, to free himself from the self-hatred which that attitude involves. Through the humiliating, and ultimately cleansing experience, the established cycle of drug addiction, theft, prison, and parole, he comes to accept the principle of hope, and begins to look into a future of survival. There are still no fucking presents under the Christmas tree, but there is the recognition of the necessity to struggle, and of the will and the power to work for a future.

Pedro Pietri is, of course, best known through his protest poetry dealing with the social situation of Puerto Ricans in New York, such as the *Puerto Rican Obituary*, his famous long poem about the dying of Juan, Miguel, Milagros, Olga, and Manuel, about the causes of their death, about the death of their lives, their mutual hatred, and about the alternative, meaningful, dignified lives they might have led under different conditions.[9] As such it constitutes a Nuyorican viewpoint within the ensemble of second culture in the U.S. The point I want to make at this juncture, however, is that of a Nuyorican poem reaching into the general human condition, under the threat of nuclear extinction, which will hit all races and nations alike.

> Whose arms
>   will we have for breakfast
> tomorrow morning?
> & whose legs
>   will we have for lunch
> if the afternoon ever comes?
> & if we are not extinct by supper time
> we can boil our eyeballs
> & have visionary soup
>   or maybe the war will
>   end soon
> & we will have something else to eat
> besides the indigestible after effects
>   on the menu
>   of a nuclear con fron tation[9a]

The poem uses the cynical form of a "prayer backwards," which, in its extremity, is compatible, and indeed correlative with the monstrosity of the nuclear catastrophe. The fact that the nuclear threat is created by people, by human beings, very logically, in the poem, leads to a string of cannibalistic images, to the eating of human parts for breakfast, lunch and supper. Some of the images have double meanings: the arms refer to the body parts as well as to the weapons; "visionary soup" simultaneously implies vision as sight (eyeballs), but also a vision as foresight of something in the future, which suggests the vision of reason and of life instead of destruction. A similar imagery occurs in a poem by the black feminist poet Melba J. Boyd, where GI soldiers are likened to "stuffed olives to be served with the limited nuclear war."[10]

> . . . thunder cracks in the
> birth of bloodied clouds
> and oil hovers
> and oil settles
> and the heads of state
> state the thirst. . . [11]

The greed of a key industry capital, distanced through the political administration as its tool, constitutes the core image in a Chicano poet's more recent contribution to international second culture in the U.S.A. Minority literature, particularly if it revolves around a specific geographical area, is in danger of being labeled "regional." Alurista's and that of several other poets of the "Chicanismo" generation, in addition, received the label "national" or "cultural nationalism." And yet it was the "poeta antropólogo,"[12] the teacher Alurista,[13] who early expanded his poetic language and his imagery into international areas. *Spik In Glyph?* manifests a further step in this development by the inclusion, for instance, of Puerto Rican Spanish and Dutch.[14]

"Borinquen" is a masterful example of arranging onomatopoeic chains and clusters of imagery around the theme of work and exploitation on the island of Puerto Rico. The location of the poem, its "time-space," as it were, is evolved through a series of sounds, a string of images, puns, ambivalent significances and associative amalgamations, contrasts and mutual enrichments of thoughts and insights.

> . . . caribe rising
> caribe cumin'
> caribe kan món
> back from the bones
> back from the stones, món

>   caribe cumin' right, cumin' left
>   cuttin' thru the loans
>   caribe cuttin' thru credit. . . [15]

The gradual registering of sound and life develops into a set of images around the cycle of nature, how the oil production cuts through this cycle; and it is with the description of the toiling workers, that the concept of Aztlán is introduced, the extension of Aztlán as it were, across the continent to the Caribbean. In the structure of the poem, the flowing of imagery away from the climactic mention constitutes its dénouement: the multinationality of monopoly capital calls for an international solidarity of exploited workers under the Amerindian roof of Aztlán.

>   . . . and working people sweat
>   throughout the land
>   throughout Aztlán
>   sin fronteras
>   no more fences, no more titles
>   no more nationality based on property
>   no more papers to show face
>   no more cards to cut the space. . . [16]

The inclusion of Estela Portillo's *Sor Juana* as the last textual example fulfills several goals. It allows the introduction of a moderately feminist perspective; it broadens the spectrum of genres; it reinforces my argument about the "inner-ethnic" Chicano/Chicana contribution to second culture by adding to former analyses, that of a very recently published example.[17]

Sor Juana is a historical play in three acts about the life and the struggle of Sor Juana Ines de la Cruz (1651-1695). The emphasis is on the last two years of her life, but several flashbacks to as early as 1659 illuminate important stages of her life history and the formation of her mind, her writings and her activities. A strong focus emerges on her relationship to her admired mentor, but also antagonist, Father Antonio Nuñez de Miranda:

> Father: Have you forgotten your beginnings? You are mejicana!
>
> Sor Juana: I will not take sides! I dream, I hope for, I work for the brotherhood of all men . . .
>
> Father: What substance is there in the words you write, the ideas you express, when in this very city you hear the sad songs of the

	Zambo slaves living in the hovels behind the rich man's house? The cry of women whose children are in pain because of hunger? Look upon the earth to find your heaven, child. It is not in pretty words . . .
Sor Juana:	I feel with you, but you must understand—I fight the same struggle. My voice carries all over, my words of love, compassion, brotherhood, peace . . .
Father:	I am speaking of human beings—not words!
Sor Juana:	You refuse to understand!
Father:	And you refuse to see!

Antonio's commitment to the victims of feudal exploitation and Sor Juana's all-encompassing spiritual and material humanism are here juxtaposed to show two equally valid variants of a radical plebeian theology. Both of them are mejicana/mejicano versions and visions of a Christian mankind versus the established colonialist Spanish system of Catholicism, whose missionary thrust harmoniously accompanied the European conquest and brutal subjugation of an indigenous people.

Structurally and historically, Sor Juana's struggle against the Spanish Catholic power system could be compared to Juan Diego's fight of getting his mejicano peasant vision of the Virgen del Tepeyac accepted by the Spanish bishops.[19] If abstracted, however, from the historical situation and translated into a more universal application, Sor Juana's hunger for knowledge and search for truth, and her proud and dignified posture of equality, could be seen as models for *all* women's struggles for equality and *all* Third World endeavors to free its peoples from ignorance and illiteracy.

Estella Portillo, in reviving Sor Juana's quest and her specific oneness/wholeness/holiness with God in the art form of her play, has revived a significant sector of the Chicana's/Chicano's own Mexican history and reintegrated it into that cultural tradition. This creative rewriting of history represents an important contribution to the Chicano democratic culture and, as such, an appropriation into part of second culture of the U.S.

The brief analysis of the first three texts has indicated that, in addition to a specific ethnic or national cultural tradition, the cross-cultural dimension may add to the ensemble of second culture in a multicultural conglomerate: the Nuyorican's identity quest as American black; the Nuyorican reaching into the anti-nuclear grass root movement of no ethnic distinction; the Chicano extending his notion of Aztlán to the exploited people of the island of Puerto Rico.

What, then, would a critical expansion of the Lenin formula of the two cultures into the present entail; could it help us to perceive processes and phenomena more sharply within the multi-ethnic cultural pluralism of the modern U.S.A.?

III. Four Dimensions of the "Two Cultures" Theory

A very condensed systematic would briefly look at the problem in four ways, the first being the level of production. Culture, in its broadest sense, had been defined as a "whole way of life."[20] Within that, the production of artifacts, a creative self-realization of man and woman, music, art, the telling of jokes in a bar, literature, would be integrated. Transitions would be gradual. Such a relationship of life to art as culture involves the community of men and women, involves help, love, solidarity and might ultimately create a collective consciousness.[21] It would involve certain rituals, moral norms and ideological values; it could be, in elements, a consciously democratic and socialist life which would crystalize into the aesthetics of a democratic and socialist culture.

The subjects, the prime movers of this kind of culture production would, however, be products of a contradictory social context. Second culture, since Lenin and in the Western world of today, only exists as a permanent and dynamic dialectic with the first. Contradictions will tear right through the feelings, the consciousness, the language, the music, the produced textual contexts of individuals.

The problem could, secondly, be looked at in terms of appropriation and reception. Second culture in the shape of artifacts or aesthetic products only exists in *elements*, in fragments. Neither in a historical, nor in a contemporary sense, does second culture, if produced under conditions dominated by bourgeois capitalist power structures, constitute continuity: the elements are either chronologically fragmented or geographically separated. Second culture creative and/or history-writing will therefore have to rescue the elements of its own history from oblivion and place them within a growing cultural tradition. In the contemporary period, the organization of second culture has to create networks of distribution and reception.

The dialectic complexity of the situation under capitalism will frequently account for the distribution and marketing of second culture products through the channels of the first. Democratic and, particularly, socialist elements may be lost in that process. On the other hand, second culture will appropriate forms and structures of the first culture, and, if successful, reshape or remodel them according to its needs or intentions. These may be forms of popular or mass culture, which will, filled with new content, reach a larger public.

The two cultures theory is, thirdly, still relevant as a concept of struggle. Since it reflects a society of different classes and races, it must not be perceived as static or horizontal, but rather as dynamic or vertical. Through the ideological qualification of its content as democratic and socialist, the transitions become fluid. Proletarian culture is not necessarily always democratic and socialist; bourgeois culture, correspondingly, not always reactionary. The radical-democratic components of bourgeois culture, for instance, are indispensable for the second-cultural united front.

In the multinational societies of high industrialization, the theory of the two cultures attains a new relevance, which it did not necessarily have in pre-Soviet Russia, with regard to the nations within nations, or the different ethnic razas. There is, undoubtedly, an ideological clash *within* the Mexican American, and the black American ethnic groups. Their self-reference, however, as "nations" or "tribes"[22] indicates, to the extent that national liberation is not chauvinistic, the second culture quality of the specific liberation struggle. The self-reference as "Third World" points to the unifying experience of an "internal" US-imperialism for the internal nations mentioned, but also clarifies the relationship to Third World nations outside the geographical boundaries of the U.S., which experience the "external" imperialism.

Legitimately, we can speak therefore of an ensemble of international second culture within the U.S., to which the Chicano and Nuyorican literatures, together with the black American and Native American literatures, contribute significant elements.

The theory is, finally, relevant as method. Juan Gómez Quiñones, who has presented the most sustained attempt of Chicano cultural theory, arrives at "three culture and identity groups, or more exactly two cultures and a subculture, the cultural poles are two: Mexicans versus Anglo United States."[23] This notion is descriptive or horizontal. It accurately describes the juxtaposition of the "historical enemies" in terms of the land, the border, the economics, etc. It omits, however, the ideological demarcation, the qualification according to content. Only the latter will be able to perceive democratic and socialist elements of the United States Anglo culture, and indeed those of other ethnic groups of color, as directly ideologically related. Vice versa, dominant traits within Mexicans could thus be identified as, potentially or in fact, kin to the first ruling culture of the Anglo United States.

As method, the two cultures theory then enables us to differentiate, to identify the contradictions, the fractures, the chasms within the chaos of imperialist cultural conditions, processes and relations, to identify elements of second culture across class and race border lines. The method applies to cul tural products as well as to their distribution and reception. It may help the creative artist in his/her self-perception and self-criticism.

IV. Conclusion

To go back to our literary examples from the beginning: in Piri Thomas' and Pedro Pietri's work, as representative of Nuyorican literature, we can identify the images of Puerto Rican experience, but also generally of Third World experience, and of the anti-imperialist struggle. The images are integrated into a dialectic of form and content, but an aesthetic surplus does also occur. Nuyorican literature, though still very much in the experimental stages of its beginnings, can be seen as universal in its meaning. If it is a literature of second culture, it is not simply protest literature. The two cultures approach does away with the prejudice of established literary criticism, whereby social theme cannot render great art. Democratic literature is universal at the same time.

Alurista has been identified as the Chicano poet who appropriated and reshaped significant elements of an ideological and mythological past, thus infusing energy and dignity into Chicano literature.[24] Others have done this in different ways, a process, characteristic of the late 60s and early 70s in Chicano literature, which is today sometimes looked at as nostalgic, romantic, self-mythologizing.[25]

The reappropriation of one's own cultural history is a long, contradictory, and sometimes painful process. There is passion involved and one-sidedness, bias. The significance of the so-called cultural-nationalist phase, "ethnocentric" as it may have been, for the formation of an anti-imperialist, democratic, and socialist ideology within the Chicano cultural movement, cannot be underestimated. It has also given us a rich aesthetic experimentation in poetry, an abundance of original metaphors.

In reaching out to Puerto Rico in the poem quoted, Alurista has, through the cluster of images encircling the theme of oil production and profit, aestheticized a crucial power and finance factor of the ruling world system. The imagery has been internationalized into all Third World second culture.

Estella Portillo Trambley has explicitly stated that her art is non-political;[26] surely correct, if one thinks of specific political issues or electoral politics. However, her Chicana contribution to a second culture of the U.S. is at least threefold:

The Chicana feminist perspective, Portillo's women protagonists are portrayed as strong-willed, self-determined individuals who reject their traditional roles, who struggle and attain dignity in tragedy. The quest, either for truth or for knowledge or for one's inner self, is generated by, and juxtaposed to, a situation of oppression or ecological destruction. One thinks here of the integration of the two plots in *Rain of Scorpions*, where on the one hand, the ecological suffocation of the people of Smeltertown is symbolized by the flood of dead scorpions, while the youngsters' search for the sacred green valley represents the quest for the spiritual homeland of the Chicanos.

The reappropriation of history, Sor Juana's struggle for equality in the world of science and letters, her humanism and passion for the people, her love for Antonio, and her struggle against him, all this is as rooted in history as it could happen today. It is a remodeling of a life out of the Mexican past for the living Chicano present.

Portillo's work, not unlike Rudolfo Anaya's, might pose a particular challenge for the two cultures approach, as the contradictions of our times very intricately manifest themselves in it.

[1] Originally published in the Russian journal *Proveshchnive* 10, 11, 12. Available in English in the fifth installment of the Progress Publisher's edition of "The Right of Nations to Self-Determination" (1971), p. 7 ff. I have worked with the German edition of Lenin's *Werke* (vol. 20), p. 8 ff.

[2] The basic idea of applying the Lenin thesis to English and American literature came out of an interdisciplinary research project at Bremen University. Cf. Bremer Forschungsprojekt: "Zur Geschichtsschreibung, Zweiter Kultur. Konturan einer Theoriebildung", in *Zweite Kultur in England, Irland, Schottland, USA*, *Gulliver* 9 (1981), 9–40; see also Thomas Metscher: "Present Significance of Lenin's Concept of Two Cultures", *Artery* VI, 2, 3 (1982), 37–40. For my own application to Chicano literature see Dieter Herms: "La literatura chicana y la teoría de las dos culturas", *Plural* XIV-II, 158 (Nov. 1984), 34–39.

[3] Lauro Flores: "Teoría de 'dos culturas' y letras chicanas", *Plural* XIV-X, 166 (Julio 1985), 44–49.

[4] Ibid., p. 46.

[5] See Wolfgang Binder: "Die Nordwanderung der Puertoricaner und ihre Literatur", in Berndt Ostendorf (ed.): *Amerikanische Gettoliteratur* (Darmstadt 1983), p. 323–355, and Dieter Herms: "Native American, Chicano, and Puerto Rican Fiction. A Survey", in Hedwig Bock and Albert Wertheim (eds.): *Essays*

on the Contemporary American Novel (Munich 1986), 355-374, esp. p. 364 ff.

[6] Piri Thomas: *Down These Mean Streets* (New York 1967); Vintage Paperback edition (New York 1974), p. XI.

[7] Ibid., p. XII.

[8] Ibid., p. 96.

[9] Pedro Pietri: "Puerto Rican Obituary", in María Teresa Babin and Stan Steiner (eds.): *Borinquen, An Anthology of Puerto Rican Literature* (New York 1974), p. 453-466.

[9a] Pedro Pietri. "A Prayer Backwards" in Miguel Algarín and Miguel Piñero (eds.): *Nuyorican Poetry. An Anthology of Puerto Rican Words and Feelings* (William Morrow, New York 1975), p. 32.

[10] Melba Joyce Boyd: "Wingless Spiders," in *Thirteen Frozen Flamingoes* (Bremen 1984, p. 12). Melba Boyd created the cross-cultural dimension at the Chicano Studies Conference in 1984, which came to be the predecessor of the Paris conference in 1986. Cf. Genevieve Fabre: "International Symposium on Chicano Culture," *Gulliver* 17 (1985), 153-154.

[11] Alurista: "Borinquen," in *Spik in Glyph?* (Arte Publico Press, Houston 1981), p. 20.

[12] See Gary D. Keller: "Alurista, poeta, antropólogo, and the recuperation of the Chicano identity," introduction to Alurista: *Return. Poems Collected and New* (Bilingual Press, Ypsilanti 1982), XI-X/IX.

[13] Cf. chapter "The Teachings of Alurista" in Bruce-Novoa: *Chicano Poetry. A Response to Chaos* (Austin 1982), 69-95.

[14] Cf. "nether, nether, netherland" or "from amsterdam" in *Return*, op. cit., 132, 134-137. Ricardo Sanchez' *Amsterdam Cantos* might also be noteworthy in this context. In the as yet unpublished 1984 poem of Alurista's, "there will be no bullfights this fall," some German occurs.

[15] "Borinquen," op. cit. p. 19.

[16] Ibid., p. 20.

[17] See Dieter Herms: "Die Literatur des Chicano Movement: Identitatssuche, Kulturkonflikt und Protest", in *Amerikanische Gettoliteratur*, op. cit. 293-322, discussing works by Anaya, Gonzalez, Alurista, Delgado, Villaseñor, Nelson, Peréz, and "La literatura chicana. . . ". op. cit., where there is a focus on . . . *y no se lo tragó la tierra, Floricanto en Aztlán, La Carpa de los Rasquachis*. Lauro Flors (in his "teoria de 'dos culturas'. . . ", op. cit., p. 47: "Mucho tiempo ha transcurrido desde aquel entonces.") criticizes that these works are too old; therefore now the focus on a very recent publication. Obviously, it is impossible to give full credit to the play, within the framework of this paper. A few pointed observations will have to suffice.

[18] Estela Portillo Trambley: *Sor Juana And Other Plays* (Bilingual Press, Ypsilanti 1983), p. 178.

[19] Cf. El Teatro Campesino, *La Virgen del Tepeyac*, San Juan Bautista.

[20] Raymond Williams: *Culture and Society 1780-1950* (Harmondsworth 1971), p. 18.

[21] What I understand by community/collective consciousness, in the context

of cultural production, and with regard to literature, is very well captured in Tomás Rivera: "Chicano Literature. The Establishment of Community", in Luis Leat et al. (eds.): *A Decade of Chicano Literature 1970-1979* (Santa Barbara 1982), p. 9-17.

[22]E.g. Nation of Aztlán, Amerindia, Nation of Islam, etc.; Anaya also calls Chicanos a "tribe."

[23]Juan Gómez Quiñones: "Toward a Concept of Culture," in Joseph Sommers and Tomás Ybarra-Frausto (eds.): *Modern Chicano Writers* (Englewood Cliffs 1979), p. 62.

[24]See Bruce-Novoa, Gary Keller, op.cit., and Tomás Ybarra-Frausto: "Alurista's Poetics—The Oral, The Bilingual, The Pre-Columbian," in *Modern Chicano Writers*, op.cit., p. 117-132.

[25]E.g. Richard A. García: "Chicano Intellectual History—Myths and Realities," in *A Decade of Hispanic Literature* (Revista Chicano-Riqueña, Houston 1982), p. 285-289.

[26]Bruce-Novoa: *Chicano Authors. Inquiry by Interview* (Austin 1980), p. 173.

The Chicana: A Marginal Woman

Marcienne Rocard
Université de Toulouse-Le-Mirail

Very early, in the wake of the Chicano movement, the Chicana realized, the urgency of self-definition, hence the mood of introspection and self-reappraisal that has pervaded Chicana literature from the first. The Chicana's attempt at self-definition and self-assertion, however, is different from that of her male counterpart while men's main concern has been asserting their existence as a group outside the barrio, women have first to achieve recognition *within* their own community. Particular emphasis is laid, in Chicano literature, on the *duality* of the Mexican-American: a choice has to be made by the problematic hero, torn between two cultures; on the other hand, that same duality allows some Chicanos to claim kindship with all Latin Americans, whereas the Chicana insists on her *minority* status. In fact, she is more than "twice a minority,"[1] as Margarita Melville views her in her book on the Mexican American woman. She, indeed, deserves this designation for *four* reasons: as woman, the Chicana experiences the universal oppression that comes from being a female; she is all the more subordinate to man as she is to the victim of a male-dominated cultural heritage; her otherness she considers a liability in white American society; as a pocha, an Anglecized Mexican woman, she finds it hard to gain admittance into the Latin Americn community at large. While images of schizophrenia predominate in Chicano literature, along, occasionally, with a more jubilant, positive symbolism, the themes of subordination and exclusion are exploited at length by the Chicana writer. Alternately sarcastic (as a means of self-defense) and diffident, in her early development, the Chicana was paving the way for a greater autonomy and bolder self-affirmation, which do not fall within the scope of this study.

Until recently the Mexican-American woman had passively confronted the image of herself offered in literature and by society, both largely dominated by men. She did bring her contribution to Mexican American literature, however, but, so to speak, in a minor key, mostly as transcriber of myths and old legends. Since the mid-seventies the Chicanas have been turning inward toward themselves. Unlike the men of their community, who could afford to be unself-centered, they have made self-reflexion the first priority. In her long epic poem "Chicana Evolution,"[2] Sylvia Alicia González relates the genesis and ordeal of the Mexican-American woman. The recurring line "yo soy Chicana" echoes the "yo soy Joaquín" of Corky Gonzales (no kin!), but whereas the latter deals with the whole of the Mexican-American people, the former's exclusive concern is Chicana "herstory." In the opening lines of *Victuum* (1976), which she terms a "classical biographical novel", Isabela Ríos describes her own birth as she is in the process of being born, thus literally and symbolically re-creating herself. The Chicana's self-recreation first starts with a refusal to let others, i.e., men, define her:

> Ya dejáte de ser cómplice
>   a ajena definición. . . .
> busca tu nombre
>   dentro de ti misma
> CHICANA
> crea tu palabra
>   tu esencia TU. . . . [3]

writes Margarita Cota-Cárdenas. However variously expressed, the search for the Chicana's "essence" rests on the assumption that she should no longer be defined as an appendage or in relation to someone or something, along genetic, ethnic, or social lines: "Mujer, ¿quién eres?" asks Virginia Cantú:

> Me describen como mujer, Chicana, student, greaser,
>   madre descuidada.
> ¿Quién soy?[4]

Significant enough is the title of Carrie A. Castro's poem "Labeling Theory":

> Call me pocha
>   and I'll cringe
> Call me crazy
>   and I'll laugh
> Call me traditional
>   and I'll doubt it
> . . . .
> Call me Carrie
>   and I'll cooperate.[5]

At stake again, in Gloria Treviño's poem, another "labeling" game, is the poet's full personhood:

No me digas ama de casa
Y no me digas esposa,
pero si menciona
¡que soy persona!⁶

In her self-analysis the Chicana writer first denounces woman's universal subordination and oppression; then, more specifically, she exposes a culture, her own, that idealized woman as the center of family life, in which any role outside of that narrow sphere was censured. This, not acculturation, is a major theme with the Chicana. In the name of her sisters, Elena Guadalupe Rodríguez laments:

the frustration of
what you are
mujer.⁷

Marcela Lucero-Trujillo denounces "the frustrations of being a woman within the sexist microcosmic Chicano world of machismo."⁸ She sarcastically debunks the cult of marianismo, or the idealization of the long-suffering, self-abnegating, morally superior, mother:

Soy la superwoman Chicana
    planchando ropa,
    lavando trastes,
    cuidando niños,
Sin decir nada.⁹

In another jocular poem, "Machismo is Part of our Culture,"¹⁰ she makes fun of her Chicano boss, bossed around by his Anglo wife, a double revenge on one guilty of machismo in the first degree.

Estela Portillo-Trambley's collection of short stories *Rain of Scorpions* may be considered as a revision of the roles of men and women, with the latter agonizingly aware of "the idiocy in the predicament of being a woman".¹¹

Though some militants, like Armando Rendón, the author of *Chicano Manifesto*, may have duly recognized female participation in the Chicano movement, most—generally men—were expected to run the show while women were to remain in the wings, that is in the kitchen:

You speak of the new way,
a new life. . . .

Pero your voice is lost to me, carnal,

> in the wail of tus hijos,
> in the clatter of dishes
> and the pucker of beans upon the stove.
> Your conversations come to me
> de la sala where you sit
> spreading your dream to brothers. . . . [12]

Quite justifiably, Lorna Dee Cervantes expresses reservations about the new American dream.

The Chicana's challenge of traditional roles appears through her own subversive use of symbolism. No longer the trustworthy keeper of the household, the Virgen of Guadalupe (to whom the Mexican woman had been habitually associated) is presented as a mundane liberator by Lydia Camarillo:

> si somos espejos de cada una,
>   Soy Malinche,
>   Soy la Virgen de Guadalupe
>   Soy Sor Juana Inés de la Cruz.
>   Soy Frieda Kahlo,
>   Soy mujer.[13]

This is an explicit blow dealt religion as an important instrument for perpetuating the subordination of women.

Blatantly missing from Chicana writings is the *cucaracha*, the double symbol of the indomitable spirit of the Mexican revolutionary and of the wretched conditions of Chicanos; as if what the Mexican Revolution had achieved and what the Chicano movement had been fighting for came only second in the Chicana's preoccupation. The garden, not the house, traditionally "woman's sphere,"[14] the real locus of power of woman, is used as a metaphor for the Chicana psyche. The prevailing mood in *Rain of Scorpions* is one of combativeness, as Portillo sets out to undermine the sex-role polarization; in all of her stories but one, woman, not man, is the chief protagonist. Her sustained sarcastic use of the garden metaphor is meant to break the traditional patriarchal order. There are two gardens in Portillo's book: one in "The Paris Gown" is ruled by the Apollonian principle of order; it is "impressive and almost manicured to perfection"[15]; it is man's garden; the other, pictured in "If It Weren't for the Honeysuckle," is woman's own; it is permeated by the irrational and the will to freedom; the honeysuckle "had grown all around the hut because of careful care; it had also become the Dionysian covering of a soul."[16] In the story "Trees," androcentrism is symbolized by the Edenic apple orchard owned by a God-ordained man, Don Teófilo Ayala, and ruled by his four

four sons.

Once outside of the home the Chicana becomes again conscious of her minority status in two ways: as a hyphenated woman she resents "the alienation of being a Chicano woman in the larger macrocosmic white male club that governs the United States"[17]; as a Chicana feminist, she is more or less ignored by the larger Anglo female liberationist movement, and by the "loyalists" of her own community who accept the traditional role.

Her basic reaction to the dominant culture differs slightly from that of her male counterpart. Lorna Dee Cervantes does lament the impact of the major language:

> Mamá raised me with no language
> I am an orphan to my Spanish name
> the words are foreign stumbling on my tongue.[18]

But never does the Chicana wield bilingualism explosively, as a weapon. Her occasional use of the two linguistic codes seems to be prompted less by a deliberate will to self-assertion and subversion than by instinct, as grandma and granddaughter in Lorna Dee Cervantes' poem, quite naturally, over breakfast, resort to whichever language they are more comfortable in:

> "¿Por qué no te quieres casar?"
> Abuelita,
>   you don't understand[19]

The Chicana's problem is never really posed in terms of a cultural choice to be made as is the case of the maturing heroes of *Pocho* or *Chicano*. In the volume aptly entitled *Morena* by Francisco Lomelí, we are presented with fifty pieces of a Chicana mind: four Chicana poets express what it means to be brown in a white society. The emphasis, however, is on their experience of being women and, as such, on their common experience of oppression and inequity. To a certain extent, the Chicana's attitude toward the dominant society is best epitomized by Estella Portillo's own decision regarding her *Morality Play* "to deal with the political in a non-political way."[20] The young Chicana remains a dangling woman, a marginal one, forever expectant as the female protagonist of Victoria Hogan's poem "Tug-of-War":

> Pushed.
> Pulled.

> I dangle between two worlds.
> One that welcomes me
>
> . . .
>
> The other pushes me out
>
> . . .
>
> I would answer
> that for the time being
> I prefer to be where I am,
> where I will remain uncertain
> and curious about them both.[21]

Significant enough, however, is Bernice Zamora's discomfort with standard English, as a language which reflects the values of white middle class males, as a "wrong language" (to use the expression of Toni Tanner, the author of *City of Words*.[22] In *Restless Serpents* the Chicana poet lashes viperously at "the lordly lords' language":

> Words, words, English words—
> turds of the golden goose—
> words we picked up, wiped off,
> cleaned up, prepared and served
> as canapés to the lordly lords. . . . [23]

Will the Chicana eventually evolve her own mode of feminine/feminist writing? Isabela Ríos' stylistic innovation in her novel *Victuum*, that is her continuous resort to "showing," with its appeal to intuition and imagination, instead of "telling," a discursive mode of narration, can hardly be seen as an intentional flouting of male discourse (both Anglo and Chicano).

A more belligerent mood prevails, nevertheless, among Chicana feminists, engaged in sexual politics against formidable odds: to begin with, they were confronted with the "loyalists" of their own group and held in suspicion as "agringadas," then they were excluded from the Anglo liberationists' club. Yet the feuds within the female community, which could have provided the Chicana writers with appropriate thematic material, are practically absent from their works, as though ethnic solidarity had proved stronger. When it comes, however, to the Anglo feminists, they fling aside all restraints. In the collection of essays edited by Magdalena Mora and Adelaida del Castillo[24] the emphasis is clearly on the baneful conjunction of capitalism and patriarchy and the way they interact to maintain the oppression of the Chicana. Because her emancipation is linked to the liberation of her people she refuses to subordinate her needs as a member of a racially oppressed group for a greater cause, the universal oppression of women, which results in her being ostracized by her Anglo sisters. Besides, both parties disagree on some specific issues (abortion, in particular), as summed up in this satirical piece by Marcela Trujillo, to which the last two lines provide an apt coda:

> Over cookies and tea
> you still sidled up to me
> and said,
> "Sisterhood is powerful"
> I said
> "Bullshit and allmotherful"
> . . .
> "no more cookies, please"
> You differentiate between the two,
> but can you really separate
> your sex from your color,
> No? Then see, it won't do.
> And, by the way,
> have you offered the campesina
> a piece of the American pie?[25]

The Chicana does not feel any closer to her "sister of the South"[26] for just the opposite reasons: because she is not brown enough:

> Heritage
> I look for you all day in the streets of Oaxaca.
> The children run to me, laughing,
> . . . .
> My brown body searches the streets
> on the dye that will color my thoughts.
>
> But Mexico gags
>   "ESPUTA"
> on this bland pochaseed,[27]

writes Lorna Dee Cervantes. At least, this feeling seems to have predominated until the 1980's. Whether this minority complex is thoroughly justified still remains to be proved. The postulate should be re-examined in the light of Latin American thought. So far we have read in Latin American literature next to nothing about the Chicano phenomenon, let alone about the Chicana.

A strain of diffidence undeniably runs through the Chicanas' utterances, a conviction that whatever credentials they may produce as pochas,

Anglocized women, they will never quite qualify to join the larger Latin American club:

> I am the Chicana
> and my sisters do not hear my plea.
> They reject me constantly.
> Sometimes they embrace me,
> Yet other times, they deny me.[28]

Placing herself in a Pan-Indian perspective, the Chicana claims not only the same racial origins as her "sisters of the flesh"[29] but also a common cultural heritage, epitomized in the Nahuatl they all once spoke:

> You
> We have never met
> yet
> we know each other
> well.
> I recognized
> your high
>   set
>   cheekbones,
> slightly rounded
>   nose,
> the deep brownness
> of your hardened face-
> soft full lips.[30]

writes Ana Castillo. By way of assurance, Sylvia Gonzales adds:

> I am the Chicana
> who knows of folk medicine and witchcraft.
> I know of Cervantes and the Spanish Language Academy
> as well as of Argentine dialects
> and Mexican slang.[31]

Founding herself upon history, she pleads for extenuating circumstances:

> I am Chicana
> but while you developed
> in the womb
> I was raped again.[32]

thus pointing to her double colonization.

Even though the Chicana identifies more closely, as woman, with

La Malinche, some uneasiness remains. Las Hijas de la Chingada lack the buoyant confidence of Los Hijos de la Chingada. Upon the whole, still by 1980, a feeling of insecurity runs through Chicana literature, pointing to the fact that the Chicana, as woman and writer, is passing through a period of transition and readjustment to a new world:

> My center is in flux
> now my womb
> is uncertain
> as it has been
> singular
> times.[33]

Both Inés Hernández Tovar's refusal to give a regular title to her poem "Sin Título" and her verse arrangement reflect her uncertain mood. Sylvia Gonzales sounds self-depreciatory too:

> What value has my verse?
> I am Chicana
> I am oblivion,
> an appendage to the universe. . . . [34]

Out of this sort of "minority complex," born from a context of oppression and inequity, the Chicana is actually, by the 1980's, developing a literature of her own. Along with the image of a colonized woman emerges that of a militant artist determined to eliminate all that keeps her from being visible and to impose a new perception of herself.

---

[1] *Twice a Minority: Mexican American Women*, (St. Louis, Mo.: C. V. Mosby Company, 1980).
[2] In: D. Fisher (ed.), *The Third Woman. Minority Women Writers of the United States*, (Boston: Houghton Mifflin, 1980), pp. 418–426.
[3] "Manifestación tardía," *La Palabra*, vol. 2, 1980, pp. 37-38.
[4] *La Palabra*, op. cit., p. 87.
[5] In: *Morena*, Francisco A. Lomelí (ed.), Santa Barbara, CA., 1980, p. 11.
[6] "Sa," *Grito del Sol*, 1978, p. 111.
[7] "Viéndote," in *Morena*, op.cit., p. 76.
[8] "The Dilemma of the Modern Chicana Artist and Critic," in: *The Third Woman* op. cit., p. 326.
[9] "Superwoman," *Grito del Sol*, 1978, p. 113.
[10] In: *Third Third Woman*, op. cit., p. 401.
[11] Berkeley, Tonatiuh International, 1975, p. 99.

[12] "Para un revolucionario," *La Palabra*, op. cit., p. 56.
[13] "Mi Reflejo," *La Palabra*, op. cit., p. 56.
[14] Cf. Nancy F. Cott, *The Bonds of Womanhood: "Woman's Sphere" in New England 1780-1835*, Yale University Press, 1971.
[15] *Rain of Scorpions*, op., p. 6.
[16] *Ibid.* p. 97.
[17] Marcela Lucero-Trujillo, "The Dilemma. . . . ", op.cit., p.326.
[18] "Refugee Ship," *La Palabra*, op. cit., p. 53.
[19] "Grandma," *Grito del Sol*, 1978, p. 38.
[20] *El Grito*, 1973, p. 6.
[21] In: *Morena*, op. cit., p. 47.
[22] *Partisan Review*, Fall 1972, pp. 609-614. (*The City of Words*, London Cape, 1971).
[23] "Let the Giants Cackle," in: *Restless Serpents*, Menlo Park, Diseños Literarios, 1976, p. 35.
[24] *Mexican Women in the United States: Struggles Past and Present*. Occasional Paper No. 2, L.A., Chicano Studies Research Center Publication U.C.L.A., 1980, p. 2.
[25] "No More Cookies, Please," in: *The Third Woman*, op. cit., p. 402.
[26] S. Gonzáles, "Chicana Evolution," in: *The Third Woman*, op.cit., p. 424.
[27] "Heritage," *Grito del Sol*, 1978, p. 37.
[28] "Chicana Evolution," op. cit., pp. 424-25.
[29] ib.
[30] "Our Tongue was Nahuatl," in: *The Third Woman*, op. cit., pp. 390-91.
[31] "Chicana Evolution," p. 425.
[32] *Ibid.* p. 421.
[33] *La Palabra*, op. cit., p. 63.
[34] "Chicana Evolution," op. cit., p. 419.

Cultural Ambivalence in Early Chicana Literature

Gloria Velásquez Treviño
University of Colorado

A recurring tendency in critical analysis which has distorted Chicana Literary expression, has been to adopt a monolithic approach to Chicano prose fiction written in English before the Chicano Movement of the 1960's. Critics such as Raymund Paredes and Juan Rodríguez reflect this inadequate assessment of early Chicana authors by classifying their work as nostalgic and assimilationist in nature. This attitude is present in Juan Rodríguez' assessment of early Chicana writers of the 1930's: "All of them actually represented a step backward in the development of Chicano prose, for they returned to the quaint representation of the Mexican and the Mexican way of life, a view very similar to and yet much simpler than that presented by María Cristina Mena some twenty years before."[1] This essay is an attempt to demonstrate that while early Chicana prose fiction often reflects an assimilationist perspective, it similarly reflects an attitude of resistance to cultural domination. An important element in my discussion of this attitude of resistance expressed by the early Chicana author is her awareness of the specific concerns particular to the minority woman's experience in the United States.

The paradigm of *cultural ambivalence* provides me with a critical framework for the interpretive assessment of early Chicana prose fiction authors. Because the concept of cultural ambivalence encompasses the complexity of the Chicano experience, it allows the literary critic to examine early narrative writers in a dynamic and dialectical manner that is historically based. It takes into consideration the contradictions of the writer's social conditions and how she resolves them. Cultural ambivalence can be defined as an attitude that expresses the diverse nature of the Chicano experience in American Society. It expresses the central dilemma of the Chicano who is conscious of being a product of both Mexican and American cultures. Cultural ambivalence characterizes the dual consciousness of Chicanos as they mediate between the values of the dominant culture and those of the minority group. It is important to understand that Chicanos have not chosen to be ambivalent but that cultural ambivalence has primarily been a result of their socio-historical position in a society which subordinates minority groups both economically and culturally.[2]

The Mexican-American War, which ended with the Treaty of Guadalupe Hidalgo, can be singled out as the point of departure in examining the emergence of cultural ambivalence. With the Treaty of Guadalupe Hidalgo, Mexicans living in the disputed territories automatically became Americans. In *Foreigners in Their Native Land,* historian David J. Weber affirms that Chicanos responded to economic and cultural subjugation by Americans with both cultural resistance and assimilation: "The reaction of the Mexican community in the Southwest—including much of the upper class—to the coming of the gringos was a mixed one, just as during the Texas revolt. Some collaborated with the enemy, some resisted, and others remained indifferent."[3] Weber further notes that this ambivalent response, which occurred during the last half of the nineteenth century, was intensified by other factors such as racial and cultural discrimination directed at Chicanos by Anglo-Americans.

Another important factor that intensified cultural ambivalence in Chicano consciousness was the intense migration from Mexico that began in the first part of the twentieth century and that has continued to the present day. It has produced a heightened awareness in the Chicano population about their Mexican cultural background and consequently serves as an added barrier to their assimilation.

The prose fiction of María Cristina Mena provides us with one of the earliest examples of the dual consciousness that characterizes early Chicana literary expression. María Cristina Mena's life and cultural background attest to her cultural ambivalence. Born in 1893, Mena migrated from Mexico at the age of fourteen with her family to the United States and later settled in New York, where she began her literary career by publishing a series of children's novelettes. The publication of María Cristina Mena's first short story in 1913 in the *Century Magazine,* a prominent New York Publication, launched her career as a writer.

While María Cristina Mena focuses her interest as a writer solely on Mexico, she is indeed conscious of her dual social position in American society. In one of her most political short stories entitled, "The Education of Popo" (1915), Mena directly interprets the Chicana experience from this dual consciousness that incorporates elements of both the dominant culture and of her sub-culture.[4] The theme of this satirical narration is the conflict that results when the value systems of Mexican culture are contrasted with those of Anglo-American culture. This conflict is posited within the context of the economic penetration of the United States into Mexico during the Mexican Revolution, and is symbolized by the relationship between the family of Governor Fernando Arriola, who represents the Mexican economy, and the Cherry family, who represent American capitalism. Mena's ideological perspective reveals her criticism of the superior/inferior relationship that exists between the cultures. This political stance is incorporated in the opening of "The Education of Popo."

It is with the characterization of the two central characters, Próspero Arriola and Miss Cherry, that Mena effectively reveals an ambivalent attitude about her cultural background and her role as a minority woman. The narrator humorously contrasts Popo or Próspero and Miss Cherry, who represent the values, customs and beliefs of their respective cultures. Popo is depicted as the "true-born caballero" of Mexican society who symbolizes the honor and respect of his country. Through caricature and irony, Popo is characterized as a comical contrast to the noble and intelligent hero "Prospero" from the Shakesperian drama, *The Tempest*. Popo's relationship to his possessive mother, Doña Elvira, who perceives him as a child, further illustrates the author's criticism of patriarchy in Mexican society, as well as the traditional role of women in Mexican society, that fosters female subordination.

The description of Popo's relationship to Miss Cherry, who functions as the stereotype of the "gringa" or the American woman, illustrates the narrator's ambivalent attitude in describing female experience. Popo's reaction to the "indifferent sisterliness" that he witnesses between Miss Cherry and her mother indicates the narrator's disapproval of the liberal values of American society that allow women more freedom. This rejection of American values surfaces in other scenes in this short story which describes Miss Cherry's behavior as being typical of a "divorced woman." Mena's ethnic consciousness does not allow her to accept totally the liberal values that exist in American society.

Similarly, María Cristina Mena's awareness of the minority woman's dual social position also consists of the criticism of female subordination in American society. In "The Eduction of Popo", Miss Cherry is characterized with the same narrow images of women that Mena uses in other stories to create her female characters. Miss Cherry is idealized as a part of nature or an object of beauty and contemplation. Mena, of course, is employ ing inversion to produce the opposite reaction from the reader about these narrow images of women. The author's feminist consciousness is further emphasized by the comparison of Miss Cherry to a saint: Miss Cherry symbolizes purity and virginity to Próspero as indicated by her last name. This image of Miss Cherry as a saint contradicts her previous characterization as the "loose" or liberal American woman.

The description of Miss Cherry's rejection of Popo further emphasizes Mena's ambivalent attitude in describing female experience. After having rescued Popo from a ravine where he disappeared out of jealousy, Miss Cherry happily tells Mr. Winterbottom, her ex-husband, that in order to calm Popo she had confessed to him that she was divorced, eleven years older than he, and that she dyed her hair. This confession is of dual significance: First, it indicates the demystification of Anglo-American culture, since Miss Cherry reveals what she is really like and, secondly, the narrow attitudes that exist about women are demystified, since Miss Cherry is not completely natural nor perfect.

The manner in which Miss Cherry rejects Popo suggests that she educates him. The education Popo receives from Miss Cherry represents the socio-economic dependency of Mexico which is considered a result of American capitalism. It is here that Mena also indicates that it is not only the Mexican male who is being educated but men in general. The narrator clearly refers to sexism in both American and Mexican cultures. The cultural contrast that occurs in "The Education of Popo" in which Mena rejects elements of both Mexican and American cultures that are oppressive to women, clearly reveals the dual consciousness of the early Chicana author.

The first half of the twentieth century witnesses the development of a Chicano middle class which expresses the ideological contradictions that characterize the dual nature of the Chicano experience. The prose fiction of Jovita González, one of the most prolific authors to appear during the first half of the twentieth century, further exemplifies the problem of cultural ambivalence. On the one hand, as a native Texas-Mexican who is immersed in the social reality of her ethnic group, Jovita González reveals her political consciousness as a writer who is committed to establishing the historical presence of the native Texas-Mexicans with a description of their customs and traditions before Anglo-American colonization, protesting Anglo-American intrusion in the border areas and promoting better images of Texas-Mexicans that will contradict the stereotypical ones already present in North American literature. On the other hand, González reveals the same ideological convictions of LULAC (League of United Latin American Citizens), one of the most prominent middle class organizations in the Southwest, which considers assimilation into American culture as the solution to the Chicano's socio-economic problems.[5]

This contradictory perspective on the part of Jovita González, which reflects an attitude of both resistance and assimilation to the dominant culture, is embedded in her two principal collections of sketches entitled "Among My People." While both collections are published under the same title and during the same year, they present two distinct views of border culture and society. The first collection of "Among My People," which appears in *Tone the Bell Easy* (1932), presents a sensitive and purely descriptive view of life on the Texas-Mexican border.[6] The border community is portrayed as a closed and cohesive social unit isolated from American culture. The author's preface to this collection creates the romantic mood which characterizes the description of the border community and of those inhabitants who are significant because of their picturesqueness.

This nostalgic tone appears in several sketches of this collection in which the narrator recounts in an autobiographical style her impressions of border life while growing up on her grandfather's ranch. In contrast to the many Chicana authors who during this period portray the grandmother as the central figure in the transmission of cultural values and traditions, González isolates the grandfather as an important link to her ethnic culture. Consequently, male experience is highlighted in this collection as a central element in the description of border life while relatively little attention is given to the contributions of women. The emphasis given to nature and to the description of the flora and fauna of the border area in this sketch, further projects the image of peaceful and pastoral environment. The character sketches that are included in this collection further perpetuate a romantic view of border society. While the central characters are described in a colorful way with particular attention given to their folkloric qualities and capabilities, they are not developed as individuals.

In the second collection of "Among My People," Jovita González presents a more dynamic view of border experience that does not limit itself solely to that which is picturesque.[7] Two sketches in this collection, "Don Tomás" and "Don José María," clearly exemplify this dynamic representation of border culture and society.

"Don Tomás" focuses primarily on the description of the character and behavior of the border ranchman or ranchero. Unlike the first collection of "Among My People," which places more attention on the ideal qualities of the border people, this collection of sketches describes the negative characteristics of the ranchero who represents a real individual and not just an idealized folkloric symbol. Hence, the description of the conflicts the border ranchman experiences within his social environment are an important aspect of his characterization. Furthermore, the narrative tone in "Don Tomás" suggests disapproval of the border patriarch whose social power and prestige, both within border society and the family structure, surpass that of the established legal systems.

In the final sketch of this collection, "Don José María," Jovita González goes beyond offering an authentic depiction of the Chicano experience in the Southwest to analyzing and interpreting reality. A critical perspective surfaces throughout the sketch about the need for changing certain aspects of her traditional border culture. Cultural ambivalence surfaces in the contrasting description of the central character, Don José María. Although a negative attitude is implied in the exaggerated description that is given of the border ranchman, Don José María similarly is characterized as being representative of a unique cultural experience in the Southwest which early Chicano authors like Jovita González are attempting to define. The narrator states: "Monotonous and uninteresting from the outside, his home was the center of border culture—not the culture of Mexico, not the culture of the United States, but a culture peculiar to the community" (p. 181). In alluding to the quality of the Chicano experience, González predates future Chicano authors like Josephina Niggli and José Antonio Villarreal who also attempt to capture in their narrative the existence of a distinct Chicano identity. Nonetheless, a limitation of Jovita González' interpretation of the Chicano experience is that more value is attributed to the upper class members of border society, such as the border ranchman who is supposed to function as the highest symbol of his culture.

An important characteristic of the narrative perspective in "Don José María" that also appears in "Don Tomás," is the author's social protest against Anglo-American colonization in the Southwest. Critical comments are directed at the bourgeois values of Don José María and his family who are greatly influenced by American values. González alludes to the negative effects of Anglo-American infiltration in the ranching communities along the Texas-Mexico border. The reader is left with a critical awareness about the effects of American values on border culture and society as well as the internal systems of oppression within traditional border culture such as those symbolized by the border patriarch.

The problem of cultural ambivalence which appears as a dominant feature in the early narrative of writers such as Jovita González and María Cristina Mena, continues to permeate Chicano prose fiction throughout the early 1960's. It is not until the advent of the Chicano Movement when Chicanos began to assess themselves politically that cultural ambivalence in Chicano artistic expression is replaced by a more assertive stance. The development of Chicana awareness in the 1970's constricts the attitude of cultural ambivalence as Chicana writers begin to adopt a new tone of self-assertion while directly confronting their oppressive social situation.

¹Juan Rodríguez, "Notes on the Evolution of Chicano Prose Fiction," *Modern Chicano Writers*, ed., Joseph Sommers and Tomás Ybarra-Frausto (Englewood Cliffs, New Jersey: Prentice Hall, 1979), p. 70.

²An interesting parallel can be drawn with the social reality of Blacks in American society. The concept of *double consciousness* developed by William E. DuBois in discussing the role of Black-Americans in the U.S. is similar to my concept of cultural ambivalence.

³David J. Weber, *Foreigners in Their Native Land* (Albuquerque, New Mexico: The University of New Mexico Press, 1978), p. 99.

⁴María Cristina Mena, "The Education of Popo," *Century Magazine*, 87, No. 5 (March, 1915), 653. All further references to this work appear in the text.

⁵This ideological perspective is exemplified in an essay written by Jovita González entitled "Latin Americans," which appears in *Our Racial and National Minorities*, ed. by Francis J. Brown and Joseph S. Roucek.

⁶Jovita González, "Among My People," *Tone the Bell Easy* (Austin: The Texas Folklore Society, 1932), X, 99. All further references to this work appear in the text.

⁷Jovita González, "Among My People," *Southwest Review*, 17, No. 2 (32), 184. All further references to this work appear in the text.

La Vida Es un Spanglish Disparatero: Bilingualism in Nuyorican Poetry

Frances R. Aparicio
University of Arizona

Due to the political struggle of Hispanics in the United States as minorities within the milieu of a dominant culture, their respective literatures are characterized by a stance of cultural differentiation and resistance *vis-a-vis* the other, the Anglo world. If one considers language as both an identity marker and a tool for defining one's identity, the mixture of Spanish and English within an individual text serves to define the writer's cultural and political position within his/her bicultural world. Puerto Rican poets in the United States are diversified in their preference for literary styles, traditions and language use. There are, however, two discernible trends among Puerto Rican poets in New York. Reflecting a variety of individual linguistic experiences, poets like Iván Silóoen, Carmen Valle, Manuel Ramos Otero and Luz Ivonne Ochart write poetry in Spanish. These poets, educated in Puerto Rico, have lived or are living in New York as professionals and share an intellectual, highly-stylized—and politically committed—literary production with their counterparts in Puerto Rico. The second group, made up of poets who were born or raised in New York, like Miguel Algarín, Tato Laviera, Pedro Pietri and Sandra María Esteves, write in English or in Spanglish, and strive to create an oral, bilingual context which reflects the popular culture and the social conditions of the *puertorriqueños* in El Barrio.[1] This second category of poetry, to which we will refer as Nuyorican poetry, is based on popular language, on the everyday speech of *la gente*. As such, it represents a response to the political oppression and discrimination on the part, among many, of the educational institutions in the United States. These Puerto Ricans in the United States, as Third World writers, voice their protest against the negative attitudes of the educated, literate upper classes in a very creative and original way: by using their "incorrect" or "vulgar" language as poetic discourse and, moreover, within a literary context, as words in print. Bilingual poetry is an antidote to this common prejudice against popular language.[2]

As Tato Laviera's "esquina dude" tell us, street language is effectively convincing speech, devoid of the rhetorical and literary expectations of the written word: "i know you understood / everything i said / i know you don't need a bilingual dictionary, what i said / can *cut* into any language."[3] This is a highly functional, pragmatic language, that grows out of the urban experience at the same time that it is needed to survive in the city; it can "cut" as sharply as a knife. In Nuyorican poetry, indeed, the word functions as a *weapon* in the political and social struggle of Puerto Ricans in New York. Consequently, this politically-charged poetic language presumes an antiaesthetic attitude. Words are not valued so much for their beauty, but for their strength: "Y mis palabras quisieran ser flores / pero son puñaladas de amor."[4] Algarín's ideal language, as his verse suggests, would ("quisieran") encompass an aesthetic element; nevertheless, because of the historical context out of which Nuyorican poetry emerges, and the necessity for socio-political struggle and cultural resistance, his actual poetic language is anti-aesthetic, but communicative and politically effective. Political anger is poured into the poem and, in turn, it stirs the reader into social consciousness and, hopefully, action.

Yet popular language in literature is not merely a political reaction. It is an expression of the ontological conflict that bilingual and bicultural writers face. These writers search for a dialect or linguistic mode that most authentically expresses their cultural, individual and social experience in the United States. The dialects of English and Spanish represent an essential element of poetic creativity. After all, it is through language that we express who we are, and that others employ to define us as well. For the bilingual Nuyorican poet, the function of language as a road to self knowledge is complicated by the number of languages that he/she uses; moreover, the bicultural experience can best be defined through the use of two languages, and each poet will express his/her own stance toward the cultural values and traditions of North American and Puerto Rican life through the poetic manipulation of English and Spanish simultaneously. Writing and reading bilingual poetry are acts of cultural differentiation and reaffirmation; this functions to such a high degree that the dialectical relationship between both languages has become a central theme for this group of poets. In Miguel Algarín's words, "The newness needs words, words never heard before or used before. The poet has to invent a new language, a new tradition of communication."[5] This new tradition is bilingual poetry and, with it, an emergent poetics of bilingualism. By "poetics" we refer to the collection of metalinguistic references to both Spanish and English as tools of poetic expression and as vehicles of the "structuring"—a term Juan Flores has coined—of the individual and collective identity of Nuyoricans.[6]

As in bilingual speech, bilingual poetry exhibits a variety of functional levels in which Spanish and English combine to create a very forceful and expressive poetic reality. First, the inclusion of an individual lexical item, or word, in a second language is a basic poetic resource for the Nuyorican poet. Poems in English like "My name is María Christina" by Sandra María Esteves, and "Café" by Tato Laviera, contain key words in Spanish that function as echoes of particular Puerto Rican realities or cultural traditions inaccessible to the English language. The words "negra," "abuela" and "el barrio," in Esteves' poem, like sacred words, evoke a gamut of emotional, physical and cultural associations. The first two allude to the matriarchal force in Puerto Rican society, while "negra" also includes the positive and effective racial denotations that such a word evokes.[7] In Laviera's "Café," only three Spanish words appear at the end: "colao," "sabor" and "café" which are repeated six times throughout the text. This reputation, in conjunction with other images, conjures the sensorial experience of smelling the tasting fresh-ground coffee. The poem ends with "sabor," a highly-charged Hispanic word which encapsulates the poet's enthusiasm for this daily ritual.

It is clear that both Esteves and Laviera have not included these Spanish words in their poems in an arbitrary fashion. These examples illustrate what Octavio Paz had described as instances of "poetic revelation," the process by which the words in the poem come to the poet from within, and are, thus, "necessary" and "irreplaceable."[8] According to Paz, the act of writing poetry is an expression of the "nostalgia for an anterior state, a state of primordial unity from which we were separated."[9] This philosophical function of poetry, universal as it is, may also explain the function of Spanish words in the poetry of Esteves and Laviera. These words are not only unique in their cultural denotations, but, more important, they function as "conjuros," as ways of bringing back an original, primordial reality—Puerto Ricanneses—from which these poets have been uprooted in a political and cultural way. Even though the use of these key Spanish concepts may reflect a vestigial bilingualism on the part of the author,[10] as elements of a poetic whole they reaffirm the Puerto Rican indigenous realities that the Nuyorican poet needs to "hang on to" in his/her search of an individual and collective identity.[11]

It is not surprising to find, inversely, that many English words within Spanish poems tend to suggest the poets' feelings of alienation and dehumanization of North America urban life. In David Hernández' "Me la buscaré," the "fire-hydrant," the only English word in the text, is transformed in the poetic imagination into "mi playa," which leads the poet to contrast the horrible summers in Chicago with the idyllic setting of his uncle's farm in Comerío.[12] In the category of bilingual texts, English words tend to function as markers of urban life and experiences, while Spanish words, as we have seen, possess a sacred function of evoking the poet's origins, without violating or de-sacralizing them. These lexical choices in Spanish serve, thus, as a vehicle of cultural memory for the poet as well as for the reader.

A second, more complex function of English and Spanish in bilingual poetry is to verbalize and resolve, at times, the oppositions between the two cultures to which the Nuyorican poet belongs. As Juan Bruce-Novoa has pointed out, this type of bilingual poetry should be defined as "interlingual" because of the tension and dynamics established between both languages:

> The mixing of two languages I call interlingualism, because the two languages are put into a state of tension which produces a third, an 'inter' possibility of language. 'Bilingual' implies moving from one language code to another, 'interlingual' implies the constant tension of the two at once.[13]

Some poets, like Sandra María Esteves, establish a dualty between the Anglo and the Hispanic heritages, and describe the feelings of displacement and marginalization derived from not totally belonging to either culture, as the title of Esteves' poem, "Not Neither," suggests. She resorts to an intrasentential code-switching to reflect the dualities instrinsic in biculturalism:

> Being Puertorriqueña Americana
> Born in the Bronx, not really jíbara
> *Not really hablando bien*
> But yet, not Gringa either
> Pero ni portorra, pero sí portorra too
> *Pero ni qué what am I?*
> Y que son, *pero con what voice* do my lips move?[14]

In this context, English and Spanish are not employed exclusively to represent each culture. Nevertheless, as Gary Keller has pointed out, the act itself of switching establishes a "foregrounding" effect which signals the above mentioned dualities.[15] The disjunctive opposition ("not really jíbara, gringa, portorra" . . . "but yet / pero sí portorra too") indicates a seemingly contradictory, interrogative and *dual* sense of being a bicultural writer ("with what voice?"). Esteves ends on a note of reaffirmation of her *puertorriqueñidad*, as seen in her political contributions to her people: "Ni soy, pero soy Puertorriqueña como ella [Lolita Lebrón]. Giving blood to the independent star / Daily transfusions into the river of La Sangre

Viva."

Tato Laviera, in "the song of an oppressor," manipulates English and Spanish in an antithetic way, creating a visual and aural poetic reality which mirrors the victimization of the poet's mother by the external forces of American capitalism and consumerism. Though the semantic interaction between both languages varies throughout the poem, the Spanish refrain, "simplemente maría," is divided into three units "simple," "mente" and "maría":

> Doña Eusebia's knees were eliminated
>   simple
> her head an army boot upside down
>   mente
> her tongue was out from exhaustion
>   marí[16]

The verses dominated by English visually mutilate the refrain into three segments. The poetic use of space, and the oral fragmentation of the refrain, when recited, suggest the physical and emotional damage inflicted on Puerto Rican working women by the capitalist system, on one hand, and by the illusions derived from blindly believing in the "American Dream" and by the fantasies created by Hispanic soap operas on U.S. Hispanic channels, on the other hand.

A third and final example of interlingualism is Luz María Umpierre's poem called "Rubbish":

> Vivo en el país de los amaestrados
>   I beg your pardon, excuse me, I'm sorry
> Fila india para coger la guagua   pisotón
>   I beg your pardon
> Ir por la calle siempre a la derecha   encontronazo
>   Excuse me
> Hablar siempre en voz baja   ¡CARAJO!
>   I'm sorry
> No dejar que un papelito se te caiga en la
> acera   FLOP
>   Excuse me
> Coger un número y esperar   ¡Colao!
>   I beg your pardon
> Estacionar a quince pies, ni uno menos,
> del fire-hydrant   ¡Déjalo ahí al frente!
> Twelve inches from the curve   ¡Párate en la curvita!
>   Excuse me

¡Caminar siempre de prisa ¡Acángana!
I'm sorry

I b-e-g yul paldon, escuismi
am sorri pero yo soy latina
y no sopolto su RUBBISH.¹⁷

Here, the poet reproduces the voice of a Latina trying to catch a bus on a busy city street. The verses alternate between English and Spanish until the final stanza, in which she expresses her intolerance towards the "rubbish" that represents the North American way of life. The English verses, except for one, constitute an apologetic discourse. "I beg your pardon," "excuse me" and "I'm sorry," are echoed throughout the poem, in contrast with the observations, expressed in Spanish, of North American city life and of its respective codes of social behavior: "Vivo en el país de los amaestrados / Fila india para coger la guagua / Ir por la calle siempre a la derecha / Hablar siempre en voz baja / No dejar que un papelito se te caiga en la acera." That the Latina is subjected to the rules of North American society is expressed in the use of an apologetic discourse in English, her public voice. At the end of the poem, though, she breaks this pattern of submission and mental colonialism: "I b-e-g yourt pardon, escuismi / am sorri pero yo soy latina / y no sopolto su RUBBISH." This variation of the apologetic discourse differs from the previous English phrases in its tone and phonetics. Reaffirming her Hispanicity, Umpierre's previous submissive attitude has turned into anger towards the North American repressive code of behavior, which she defines as "rubbish." The change of attitude is signaled by the ironic use of a Hispanicized English, in conjunction with a final expression of her true feelings towards the dominant culture, verbalized in Spanish. The last word, "Rubbish," is in English because this "basura" is, after all, "gringa." These three texts—Esteves', Laviera's and Umpierre's—illustrate the diverse context in which interlingualism can function in poetry. Many more examples permeate both Chicano and Nuyorican literature. The poems of Alurista and Tato Laviera could be considered the most sophisticated instances of poetic dialogue and tension that can be achieved by combining Spanish and English within an individual poetic text.

At the stylistic level, the use of English and Spanish within a poem represents a new means through which the Nuyorican poet can experiment with linguistic play and creativity. For instance, the basic poetic technique of repetition or reiteration can be constructed using both languagues, thus redoubling the expressive force of the poet's message. In "There is Nothing New in New York," Miguel Piñero employs this technique in order to augment the impact of his words: he exhorts the reader to demystify the image of New York City as a haven of economic and social opportunities by negating the "newness" included in its name: "No hay nada nuevo en nueva york / There is nothing new in New York / I tell you in English / I tell you in spanish / the same situation of oppression."[18] The Hispanic refrain underlying this text, "No hay nada nuevo bajo el sol," and its English equivalent, "There is nothing new under the sun," establish a polysemy on the word "nuevo"/"nuevo": the "new" which is absent or negated, that is, social changes and opportunities for the *puertorriqueños*, and the "new" which makes up the city's name, New York, which, historically—and ironically—found its name because it represented a new land for the English pilgrims, victims of religious and political persecution in the Old World.

Another sophisticated use of repetition, anaphora, is present in Pedro Pietri's "Puerto Rican Obituary."[19] At the end of this poem on cultural genocide, the poet invites the reader to create a collective cultural "space" of autonomy, dignity and love, configured by the positive values of the Hispanic tradition: "Aquí se habla español all the time / Aquí you salute *your* flag first / Aquí there are no dial soap commercials." The ubiquitous "aquí" is not just a stylistic resource; it does not refer, either, to a particular location, like New York or San Juan, but to a utopian state of mind that could be created regardless of one's place of residence. As the poet concludes, aquí to be called negrito y negrita / Means to be called 'LOVE'."

Laviera's "A Sensitive Bolero in Transformation (for Anne Sexton)" illustrates how one word in two languages can form the basis for poetic dialogue as well as for word play and phonic variations. Laviera responds to Anne Sexton's poem, "The Breasts," and proposes the Spanish word and concept "seno" as an alternative to Sexton's objectification of her own body.[20] This poem is based on the connotative differences between the Spanish word "seno" and its English equivalent, "breast." Laviera exploits the phonic value of "seno" in which the sibilant *s* and the vibrant nasal *n* suggest the softness and sensuality of the represented object:

se	no	breast	seno	suave
se	no	breast	seno	sensual
			seno	orgánico
se sensual				
no	se			
suspiro		breast		
		hard		
		duro		

153

>   mistreated
>   maltratado
>   manoseado (. . . .)

In contrast, the word "breast" echoes the hardness of Sexton's images through the presence of reiterated occlusive and explosive consonants. Laviera's text can be further analized as a three-level response to Sexton's poem: first, in its linguistic and phonic echoes; second, as the poetic response of a Latino poet to a North-American poet and, lastly, as a man reading the work of a woman. In this last context, Laviera's response to Sexton's reified image of her body is one of a celebration of the woman's body through a positive and sensual poetic vision, thus proposing a series of sexual, psychological and cultural divergences between both texts.

Laviera's sensitive and witty manipulation of both languages is not limited to some selected poems. This playful—yet serious—attitude toward both languages abounds in all his poems. The titles of his last two books, *Enclave* and *AmeRícan*, are wonderful examples of the simultaneous double reading that a great poet like Laviera can achieve by fusing English and Spanish meanings into one signifier. *Enclave*, which significantly translates as "in code," contains two readings; first, *en clave* in Spanish, which suggests the musical and oral "keys" or traditions from which Laviera's poetry springs forth: "la bomba, la plena, Afro Puerto Rican poetry, Spanish declamatory rhetoric, the danza, the canción jíbara, and salsa," to name but a few.[21] In English, "enclave" refers to the colonial state of the *puertorriqueños* in New York, thus anticipating the political overtones and social criticism which is an integral part of Laviera's work. *AmeRícan*, on the other hand, has two readings in English. The basic word, disregarding its capital letters and written accent, would read "American," as in a person whose origin is America (either North, Central, or South). A second reading implies a more specific nationality: "Am-e-Rícan" ("I'm a Rícan"), that of the Puerto Rican national identity within the context of the United States society. This dual reading serves as a signifier of the bicultural world of Laviera, as well as of the "Americasization" and internationalization towards which his poetry strives. In fact, as Juan Flores has pointed out,

> Yet, as is clear from the neologistic title "AmeRícan," Laviera is intent on reaching beyond the New York enclave. He seeks to stake a claim for Puerto Rican recognition before the whole U.S. society, especially as Puerto Ricans are by now clustered in many cities other than New York. He is goading the society to come to terms with the "Rícan" in its midst, arguing through puns and ironic challenges that he will not be an American until he

can say "Am-e-Rícan" and be proud of it.[22]

Other excellent examples of bilingual word play can be found in the works of Víctor Hernández Cruz.[23] In "Financial Report" in particular, the poet presents the discourse of U.S. economics merged and confused with Hispanic words such as *plátano*, *lata* and *plata*. These Spanish words flow throughout the poem connected by one phonic difference in a syllable or by the presence or absence of a consonant. In a context of sharp criticism of United States society, Hernández Cruz creates a poetic discourse in which the word "plata" in Spanish, meaning "money" and "silver," functions as the axis for linguistic play and associations: plata—lata—plains—pains—plaza—plata-forms— plátanos. Moreover, Hispanic words are also suggested or evoked as a sub-text of certain Spanglish verses in the poem. These find their origins in Spanish colloquialisms, as in "They put fire to the lata / Flame to the can," which comes from "darle fuego a la lata," or, in the beginning of the poem, when the poet says "No, no get plata free / Only *lata* give here translated plains," which echoes the Spanish expression "dar lata," that is, to create problems or difficulties or to talk too much. The Hispanic discourse underlying this bilingual "nonsense" reveals the values of falseness, difficulties and lies of which Cruz accuses U.S. economics.

As Laviera's and Hernández Cruz's poems illustrate, puns and linguistic play are profoundly linked to committed and serious statements about bilingualism and biculturalism. This poetry expresses the particular self-consciousness of bilingual writers, their attitudes towards the problems and advantages of speaking two languages while it also explores the poetic possibilities of both Spanish and English. This metalinguistic discourse has become a recurring theme in Nuyorican poetry and, as such, represents an essential part of a nascent poetics of bilingualism.

A basic dissatisfaction of bilingual poets is against the linguistic prejudice which victimizes them and their community. As Pietri cynically states, "Manuel / Died hating all of them / Juan / Miguel / Milagros / Olga / Because they all spoke *broken* english / More *fluently* than he did."[24] The linguistic hegemony of the dominant culture results in the distortion of values and priorities by the oppressed communities. Ironically, linguistic prejudice stems from both Hispanics as well as Anglos. On the one hand, Nuyoricans are subjects to ridicule for their "broken English"; but at the same time, they are also victimized by the purist attitudes of Puerto Ricans on the island. As Fernández Fragoso puts it, "mi hija nunca a ido (a Puerto Rico)/ aprende el español para que no detecten / la otra mitad."[25]

Laviera's attitude towards this prejudice is much more challenging and aggressive than that of other poets. If in "graduation speech" he speaks with self-directed irony and humor as an "alingual" Hispanic, in "brava" he voices his anger at the linguistic prejudice stemming from the *puertorriqueños*:

> . . . y le dije
> all the spanish words
> in the vocabulary, you
> know which ones, los que
> cortan, and then i proceeded
> to bilingualize it, i know
> yo sé that que you know
> tú sabes que yo soy that
> i am puertorriqueña in
> english and there's nothing
> you can do but to accept
> it como yo soy sabrosa
> proud.

He defies this prejudice with the language of violence:

> como
> dímelo aquí en mi cara
> offend me, atrévete, a menos
> que tú no quieras que yo te meta
> un tremendo bochinche de soplamoco
> pezcozá that's gonna hurt you
> in either language. . . . [26]

In this text, the apparent incoherence created by the code-switching is in fact a linguistic echo of the woman's affirmation of her bilingual identity. It duplicates her anger, thus intensifying the impact of her message.

For some Nuyorican poets, such as Miguel Algarín, the fact that English is their tool of poetic expression creates an epistemological as well as a political conflict:

> if the man owns the world
> oh white power hidden
> behind every word i speak
> . . . if all my talk is borrowed
> from his tongue then i want
> hot boiling water to wash
> out my mouth i want lye

> to soothe my soiled lips
> for the english that i
> speak betrays my need to be
> a self-made power.[27]

How can a poet whose thoughts and feelings stem from the cultural reality of the Hispanic world define and express those ideas in the alien language? In Sandra María Esteves' words, "I speak the alien tongue/in sweet borinqueño thoughts."[28] The irony of these references to English as an "alien" tongue is that they are expressed, indeed, in English and not in Spanish. Is English really "alien" to these poets, or do they think, feel, and live in Spanish?

Tato Laviera offers a poetic solution to this linguistic dilemma. He finds a reconciliation in his acceptance of Spanglish as his tool of expression and as an identity marker for his *neo-puertorriqueñidad*. In "the patria in my borinquen" he expresses an acceptance of his bilingual and bicultural reality through an image of physical union with "la patria," his "puppy love," a union that results in a "transformed puertoricanness."[29] Laviera also sings, in a very ironic poem, to the strength of the Hispanic heritage and, specifically, to the Spanish language.[30] He praises the Spanish language for refusing to die throughout history, yet he finds the origin of this strength in the "nativeness of the spanish, / mixing with the indians and the blacks, / who joined hands together, / to maintain your precious tongue" and in the "stubbornness of the elders, / refusing the gnp national economic language, / not learning english at the expense of / much poverty and suffering." He accuses Spain of not offering her "maternal support" to Hispanics in the United States who have resisted total linguistic assimilation despite all stigmas. The irony resides in the fact that the poem is in English, and in that Laviera does not personally identify with the historical reality of Spanish as an imposed language. Nevertheless, in *AmeRícan*, his praise of "Cuban" language is quite positive. Similar to the ideas of José Vasconcelos, who saw in *mestizaje* a true source of cultural strength and survival, Laviera considers his own *mestizaje* as a Nuyorican a double source of knowledge, creativity and life. Particular words that constitute popular speech, such as "asimilao," mirror the attitudes of cultural resistance to the Anglo way of life, which characterizes the Spanglish-speaking people. According to Laviera, "déles gracias a los prietos / que cambiaron asimilado al popular asimilao."[31]

Like the "grafiteros" of New York, who are documenting and preserving Spanglish on the pages of the subway walls, Nuyorican poets are, indeed, "guerrilleros del silencio."[32] They are developing an idiosyncratic poetic form which maintains and documents the speech of the Puerto

Rican community in New York; it is, thus, a reaffirmation of the Hispanic heritage. Like an antidote to the much discussed possible disappearance of Spanish in the United States, bilingual poetry serves as a barrier against the adulteration of our perception of ourselves and of the world around us. Finally, the process of writing and reading bilingual poetry is a means of linguistic reflection, a space in which the dualities within, and the shifting realities without, can be reconciled permanently in writing, as collective memory for the generations to come.

[1] Alfredo Matilla, in " 'The Broken-English Dream': Puerto Rican Poetry in New York," *The Intellectual Roots of Independence: An Anthology of Puerto Rican Political Essays*, Eds. Iris M. Zavala and Rafael Rodríguez (New York: Monthly Review Press, 1980): 299, has categorized Puerto Rican poets in New York into two groups: "those who write in English—born or at least raised in the United States—and those who write in Spanish, "birds of passage" in the city or people who opted for temporary exile." The case of Luz María Umpierre does not totally fit into this paradigm; she is a professor of Spanish at Rutgers University, yet her poetry better reflects the Spanglish and the bicultural world of the second group of poets, rather than the first.

[2] Bilingual poetry is not a new form. It has developed during historical periods in which two cultures have merged geographically or politically. Cf. Tino Villanueva, "Introduction," *Image* 1.1 (1984): vii–xxxvii.

[3] "esquina dude" appears in Tato Laviera's *AmeRícan* (Houston: Arte Publico Press, 1985): 58-9. Alfredo Matilla, 301, also describes the non-academic and "street" origins of the language of Puerto Rican poetry in New York as "Language pulled out of the asphalt, out of experience in perpetual motion," and adds that "for the first time the industrial proletarian masters the machinery of letters. The Puerto Rican poetry of New York has no academic antecedents in the Island. Its poetic roots are in music (both Puerto Rican and Black), in 'jive,' in the streets, the subway, the barrios."

[4] Miguel Algarín, "Je me souviens," *On Call* (Houston: Arte Publico Press, 1980): 53-5. This poem is a trilingual text in which the poet presents the parallel situation of bilingualism in Canada, the linguistic dominance on the part of the English sector, and the cultural resistance exhibited by the French. As to the motif of the word as weapon, it is quite common in Nuyorican poetry. Cf. Also Algarín's poem "Flash," *On Call*, 7, in which words are associated with the violence of knives.

[5] "Introduction: Nuyorican Language," in *Nuyorican Poetry: An Anthology of Puerto Rican Words and Feelings*, Eds. Miguel Algarín and Miguel Piñero (New York: William Morrow and Co., 1975): 9. Algarín's statement coincides with Octavio Paz' view on language as an epistemological vehicle for man: "La palabra es el hombre mismo. Estamos hechos de palabras. Ellas son nuestra única realidad o, al menos, el único testimonio de nuestra realidad. No hay pensamiento sin lenguaje, ni tampoco objeto de conocimiento: lo primero que hace el hombre frente a una realidad desconocida es nombrarla, bautizarla." *El arco y la lira* (México: Fondo de Cultura Económica, 2a ed., 1967): 30.

[6]Cf. Juan Flores, "Que assimilated, brother, yo soy asimilao" The Structuring of Puerto Rican Identity in the U.S." Paper presented at the Conference on Popular Culture, National Identity, and Migration in the Caribbean, February 19-21, 1984, the University of Florida, Gainesville, Florida; published as " 'Que assimilated brother, yo soy asimilao': la estructuración de la identidad puertorriqueña en los Estados Unidos,' " *Casa de las Americas* 26.152 (1985): 54-63.

[7]Sobre el vocablo "negro," Efraín Barradas, en su Introduc ción a *Herejes y mitificadores* (Río Piedras, Puerto Rico: Ediciones Huracán, 1980): 19, ha comentado lo siguiente: "La clave del poema estáen la palabra negra, término afectivo hispánico donde Esteves encuentra todas las cifras para entenderse como ser perteneciente a un grupo social y donde además halla un bastión de defensa frente a la cultura opresora."

[8]Paz, pp. 45,54.

[9]Paz, p. 136.

[10]John Lipsky, in his "Spanish-English Language Switching in Speech and Literature: Theories and Models," *The Bilingual Review* 9.3 (1982): 191-212, refers to three types of bilingual texts, of which the first type coincides with our description: "Type I is the monolingual text, perhaps with a handful of L_2 words thrown in for flavor. Much Chicano and Boricua poetry written entirely in English falls into this category and does not necessarily presuppose a high degree of bilingualism, although biculturalism is clearly assumed," 195. A text like Laviera's "savorings, from piñones to loíza," (*La Carreta Made a U-Turn*, 45), illustrates Lipsky's comment on this function of Spanish words. Nevertheless, Spanish words, we believe, go beyond the function of creating a tone or Hispanic "flavor" to the poem. Esteves' poem is a good example of the cultural value of Spanish lexicon selected by the poet.

[11]Efraín Barradas, *Herejes y mitificadores*, 23, explains: "ciertas palabras en español funcionan en esta poesía como puntos de apoyo que, como objetos proustianos, pueden servir al poeta para reconstruir su personalidad individual y, muchas veces, colectiva." Alfredo Matilla, describes Spanish words in English poems with a similar metaphor: "lapses into Spanish are frequent, as if to rest the writer's foot on his Puerto Rican floor," 300.

[12]"Me la buscaré," *Herejes y mitificadores*, 91. See also in this anthology Víctor Fernández Fragoso's poems "El vuelo del viernes" and "Zapatié en cada una de tus esquinas," in which English words such as "uptown," "downtown" and "upstate" also reflect the influence of Anglo concepts in the Nuyorican's perception of space.

[13]"The Other Voice of Silence: Tino Villanueva," *Modern Chicano Writers*, Eds. Tomás Ybarra-Frausto and Joseph Sommers (New Jersey: Prentice-Hall, 1979): 133.

[14]*Tropical Rains* (African Caribbean Poetry Theater, 1984); taken from *Nuyorican Readings*, assembled by Juan Flores, New York, Centro de Estudios Puertorriqueños, Hunter College, 1984.

[15]"The Literary Stratagems Available to the Bilingual Chicano Writers," *The Identification and Analysis of Chicano Literature*, Ed. Francisco Jiménez (New York: The Bilingual Press, 1979): 263-316.

[16]"The Song of an Oppressor," *La Carreta Made a U-Turn* (Houston: Arte

Publico Press, 1979): 28–30; also in Barradas, *Herejes y mitificadores*, 138–44.

[17] "Rubbish," *Herejes y mitificadores*, 108.

[18] "There is Nothing New In New York," *Nuyorican Poetry*, 67.

[19] *Puerto Rican Obituary* (New York: Monthly Review Press, 1973). Other examples of poetic reiteration are Laviera's "song of an oppressor," in which the poet draws a parallelism between his mother and the soap-opera character Natacha: "natacha is you eres tú eres tú eres túó; and in "Jesús Papote," *Enclave* (Houston: Arte Publico Press, 1981), the repetition of "my name is jesús papote" emphasizes the biographical tone of the poem. In this long poem, anaphora and repetition are commonly used (i.e., "death la muerte," "mami mami," "we, nosotros," and "with the permission of. . . . ").

[20] "A sensitive bolero in transformation (for anne sexton)", *La Carreta Made a U-Turn*, 26–7. Cf. Anne Sexton, *Love Poems*, Boston, Houghton Mifflin Co., 1967, 4–5.

[21] Juan Flores, "Keys to Tato Laviera," Prologue to *Enclave*, 5.

[22] "Qué assimilated, brother, yo soy asimilao. . . . " 22–3.

[23] "Art This," by Víctor Hernández Cruz, also contains instances of bilingual word play, "She had a frenesi / A friend in C / A friendinme," as well as humorous comments on the playful elements of literal translations: "José y fina means José and thin or sounds / like oficina like José office also it had / Something in it of José is fina José is finis finished no /" or "To top it off Pepa also means pit / you see what is inside of fruits this / Is all in Spanish and something is being / lost in the translation just like you lose / your natural color when you leave a tropical / country and come to a city where the sun / Feels like it's constipated ask Lucy Comancho / she knows about all this / Art this / artis."

[24] *Puerto Rican Obituary.*

[25] "El vuelo del viernes," *Herejes y mitificadores*, 57–9.

[26] "brava," *AmeRícan*, 63.

[27] "Inside Control: my tongué," *Nuyorican Poetry*, 58.

[28] This idea was suggested to me by Eliana Rivero, who discusses the problem of the English-speaking Hispanic poet both in Nuyorican and Chicano literature. Cf. "Hispanic Literature in the United States: Self-Image and Conflict," *International Studies in Honor of Tomás Rivera*, Ed. Julián Olivares (Houston: Arte Publico Press [Revista Chicano-Riqueña 13.3] 1985). Efraín Barradas, affirms that the problem of language as a tool of poetic expression is commonly discussed by Hispanic poets who write in English and in Spanish. For those who write in English, though, this problem acquires a more profound political dimension, *Herejes*, 25. Cf. Sandra María Esteves, "Here," *Yerba Buena*, Greenfield Review, 1980.

[29] "The patria in my borinquen," *Enclave*, 50.

[30] "Spanish," *AmeRícan*, 33.

[31] "Asimilao," *AmeRícan* 54. The word "asimilao" exemplifies both cultural resistance and phonetic asimilation. It's ending *lao* is phonetically described as the "assimilation" of a consonant between two vowels; and is frequent in popular, and especially Black, Spanish. This ending, for Laviera, is untranslatable in English: "but the sound LAO was too black / for LATED, LAO could not be trans*lated*, assimilated."

[32] Laviera, "garfiteros," *AmeRícan*, 52.